STUDIO COMPANION SERIES

3D DESIGN
BASICS

BOOK THREE

STUDIO COMPANION SERIES

DESIGN BASICS/BOOK ONE

DRAFTING BASICS/BOOK TWO

3D DESIGN BASICS/BOOK THREE

PRESENTATION BASICS/BOOK FOUR

STUDIO COMPANION SERIES

3D DESIGN BASICS

BOOK THREE

DONNA LYNNE FULLMER
IIDA, IDEC

FAIRCHILD BOOKS
NEW YORK

Fairchild Books

An imprint of Bloomsbury Publishing Inc

175 Fifth Avenue   50 Bedford Square
New York   London
NY 10010   WC1B 3DP
USA   UK

www.fairchildbooks.com

First published 2013

Library of Congress Cataloging-in-Publication Data
A catalog record for this book is available from the Library of Congress
2012945338
ISBN: PB: 978-1-60901-098-0

Typeset by Tom Helleberg
Cover Design by Carly Grafstein
Printed and bound in the United States of America

CONTENTS

vii PREFACE
ix HOW TO USE THIS BOOK
xi ACKNOWLEDGMENTS

ONE – PARALINE DRAWINGS

2 OBJECTIVES
3 INTRODUCTION
6 AXONOMETRIC
  7 Isometric
    9 *Exterior Isometric*
    17 *Interior Isometric*
25 OBLIQUE DRAWINGS
  27 Plan Oblique
  34 Elevation Oblique
37 EXERCISE
39 SUMMARY

TWO – ONE-POINT PERSPECTIVE

40 OBJECTIVES
41 INTRODUCTION
43 ONE-POINT PERSPECTIVE
  45 Creating a One-Point Perspective
  46 Drafting a One-Point Perspective
  54 One-Point-Perspective Drawing
79 ADDING ROUND OBJECTS
82 EXERCISE
85 SUMMARY

THREE – TWO-POINT PERSPECTIVE

86 OBJECTIVES
87 INTRODUCTION
88 TWO-POINT PERSPECTIVE
  90 Creating a Two-Point Perspective
  92 Drafting a Two-Point Perspective
  112 Two-Point-Perspective Drawing
135 EXERCISE
139 SUMMARY

FOUR – MODEL-BUILDING TOOLS AND SUPPLIES

140 OBJECTIVES
141 INTRODUCTION
142 CUTTING TOOLS
  143 Craft and X-acto Knives
  145 Utility Knives
  146 Other Knives
  147 Rotary Cutters
  147 Circle Cutters
  148 Foam-Core Board Cutting Tools
    148 *Rabbet Cutter*
    148 *Bevel or 45-Degree Cutter*
    149 *FoamWerks*
  152 Other Cutting Tools
    152 *Mighty Cutter*

152 *The Chopper*

153 *Razor Saw and Miter Box*

154 SELF-HEALING MATS

155 METAL CORK-BACKED TRIANGLES AND RULERS

156 BUILDING MATERIALS

156 Paper

157 Boards

157 *Foam-Core Board*

158 *Museum Board*

158 *Chipboard*

159 OTHER BUILDING MATERIALS

159 Balsa Wood and Basswood

160 Acetate and Dura-Lar

160 Plastic

160 Metal

161 SUPPLIES

161 Tacky Glue

162 Glue Sticks and Adhesive Runners

162 Hot-Glue Guns

162 Drafting Dots and Tape

162 Double-Sided Tape

163 Bone Folder

164 Tool Storage

165 SUMMARY

FIVE — MODEL-BUILDING STRATEGIES

166 OBJECTIVES

167 INTRODUCTION

171 RIP-AND-TEAR MODELS

173 Creating a Rip-and-Tear Model

175 WHITE MODELS

177 Creating a White Model

181 FINISH MODELS

183 Creating a Finish Model

187 EXERCISE

191 Cut-Piece Strategy

195 SUMMARY

196 APPENDIX

197 Orthographic Drawings

199 BASIC METRIC CONVERSION TABLE

201 INDEX

PREFACE

The overall idea for this series came from the love of teaching the
freshman design studio. What I have seen time and time again is a
lack of basic design skills due to the influx of new technology, which
students often rely upon in place of hand skills. While I believe in being
a well-versed designer, the computer is just one tool in the arsenal that
a student, and a professional, can bring to the table when it comes to
designing. To this end, I believe hand skills, and the teaching of hand
skills, has become a lost art.

I tell students that beginning the study of architecture and design is
like starting kindergarten again because we ask them to learn to write
and draw in a new way. The books in the Studio Companion Series
acknowledge this and act as an introduction to skills through interactive
lessons for each topic. I have seen firsthand how students increase their
skills more rapidly by doing, rather than just by seeing. In addition, like it
or not, students today want information quickly and easily digestible.
This book's format, with numerous images and text that is direct and
simple to read, will play to this audience of future designers.

The Studio Companion Series includes four books that address all the skill sets and topics discussed when beginning the study of architecture and design. Each book is compact and highly portable and addresses topics in a clear-cut and graphic manner. They have been developed for today's students, who want information "down and dirty" and presented in an interactive way, with simple examples on the topics. The series includes: *Design Basics, Drafting Basics, 3D Design Basics,* and *Presentation Basics.*

Students are bombarded with three-dimensional images and objects every waking hour. The ability to create similar images or objects is an invaluable skill for a designer. This book will address how to draw several types of three-dimensional drawings, as well as basic physical model-building skills. While computers and other technologies have made drawing easier, students need to know how to produce these drawings quickly and on demand. They also need to be able to explore massing, form, height, and material in the swift and concise way that physical model building allows.

This book is the result of years of teaching students all over the country and listening to their questions when they were using standard textbooks.

HOW TO USE THIS BOOK

||||||||||||||||||||||||||||||||||||||||||||||||||||||||||||||||||||||||||||||||||||||||||||||||||||||||||||||||||||||||

The orthographic drawings referred to throughout this book can be found in the Appendix. Letters are used on the floor plan to indicate length and width, while numbers are used to indicate the heights on the elevations and sections. This is intended to orient you as you work through each step to complete all of the drawings.

The floor plan includes a North arrow, as discussed in *Drafting Basics,* Book Two of the Studio Companion Series. This will also assist with orientation as you create your drawings. Something to be noted is that names of drawings indicate the direction from the viewer's vantage point. This means that the north elevation of the exterior of a building will be the south interior elevation. This can get confusing, but simply think about where you would be standing to see that drawing and whichever direction your toes are pointing will be the name of the drawing.

The included orthographic drawings are produced at a $\frac{1}{8}$" = 1'-0" scale. It is recommended that you make copies of the drawings so that you can write on them as you complete the exercises included in the book.

ACKNOWLEDGMENTS

The Studio Companion Series represents the result of working with students all over the country and the thrill I get watching the "lightbulbs go off" as they learn. There is nothing like seeing a student draw a perspective properly for the first time—for me it is an addiction to be a part of this type of learning. To all my students, thank you for giving me that charge and making me proud!

Two students specifically, Victoria Beaulieu and Jacinta Stecklein, helped with this book and deserve to be singled out. They are great students and friends. Thanks to Victoria for beginning the illustrations seen throughout the book, and to Jacinta for her help with the models. Your work is appreciated very much.

From a high school English teacher to the men and women I work beside every day, thank you for showing me how to listen to students and respond respectfully while maintaining the authority in the classroom.

Finally, everyone writes and says this, but I owe my career to my supportive and loving family that has taught me things you could never find in a textbook.

STUDIO COMPANION SERIES

3D DESIGN
BASICS

BOOK THREE

ONE

PARALINE DRAWINGS

OBJECTIVES

You will be able to identify and successfully create:

- Axonometric drawings, specifically isometrics
- Two types of oblique drawings

Paraline drawings are three-dimensional drawings that allow us to look at a space from a particular vantage point. They enhance orthographic drawings—plans, elevations, and sections—because they indicate how each relates to the space as a whole. Paraline drawings are easy to create and are all drawn to a measurable scale, using drafting tools, to show an accurate representation of the space.

To fully understand all of the paraline drawings, as well as the two-dimensional drawings presented in *Drafting Basics,* Book Two of the Studio Companion Series, this small one-bedroom cabin will be used throughout the text. Orthographic drawings for the cabin, which you will frequently refer to for measurements throughout this book, are located in the Appendix.

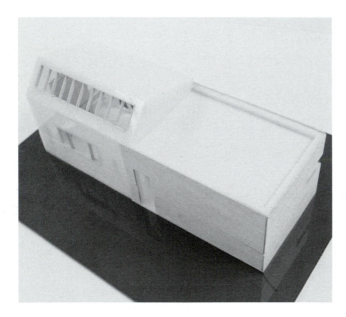 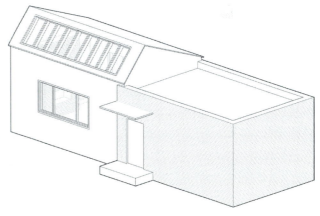

Photo and isometric drawing of cabin.

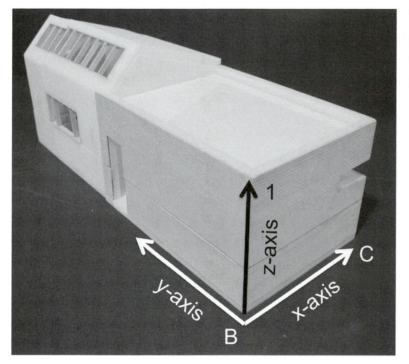

There are two major categories of paraline drawings: axonometric and oblique. Regardless of the category, all paraline drawings have:

- Lines that are parallel along the x, y, and z axes as they relate to the original orthographic drawings.

- Measurements that can be taken directly from the orthographic drawings and translated, to a measurable scale, to create the paraline drawings.

- No reference to the viewer within the space; a viewer sees the drawing as an observer outside the space, either above or below.

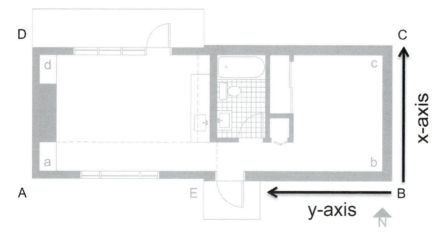

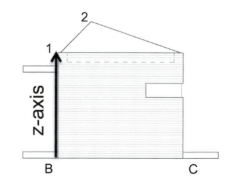

Anatomy of a paraline drawing.

AXONOMETRIC

There are three types of axonometric projection drawings: isometric, diametric, and trimetric. A trimetric of a cube is drawn with perpendicular walls shown at different angles and with unequal lengths. A diametric uses the same angle, width, and length on both sides, but not the same height. An isometric uses equal angles, usually 30 degrees, and the width, depth, and height of the cube are all the same.

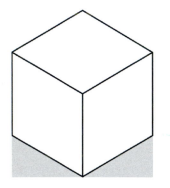

ISOMETRIC

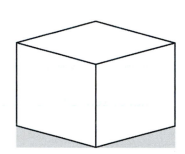

DIAMETRIC

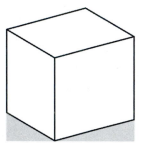

TRIMETRIC

ISOMETRIC

The most common axonometric projection drawing is an isometric, and it is the focus of this portion of the chapter. An isometric indicates:

- The size and shape of the space or object, including the overall length, width, and height.

- All of the items that the designer wants the viewer to see. An isometric can be drawn:

  - Without a wall or plane so that the viewer can clearly see inside the overall space.

  - As a plan or section view.

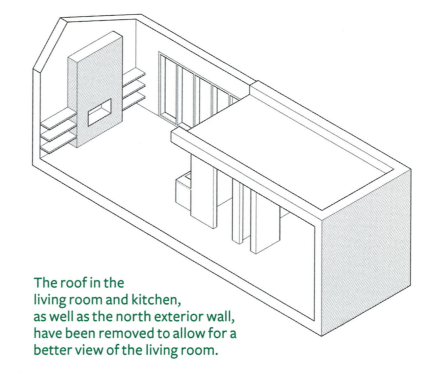

The roof in the living room and kitchen, as well as the north exterior wall, have been removed to allow for a better view of the living room.

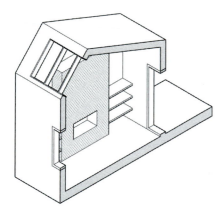

The building has been cut about 6'-0" in front of the fireplace wall to show the fireplace and shelving, as well as the windows and skylights.

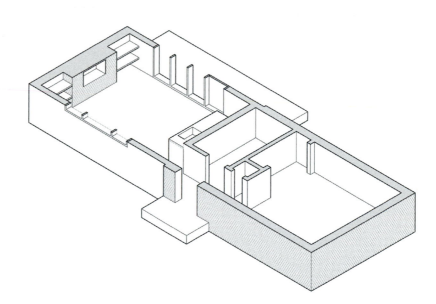

The building has been cut at 4'-0" above the finished floor to expose the fireplace, shelving, kitchen cabinets, and walls for the bathroom, bedroom, and two closets.

To create an isometric:

- Select which area of the orthographic drawing should be seen in the isometric.

- Determine the x, y, and z axes of the space you want to draw.

- Measure the orthographic drawings and use those dimensions to create the isometric drawing.

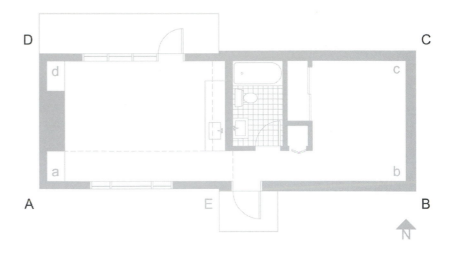

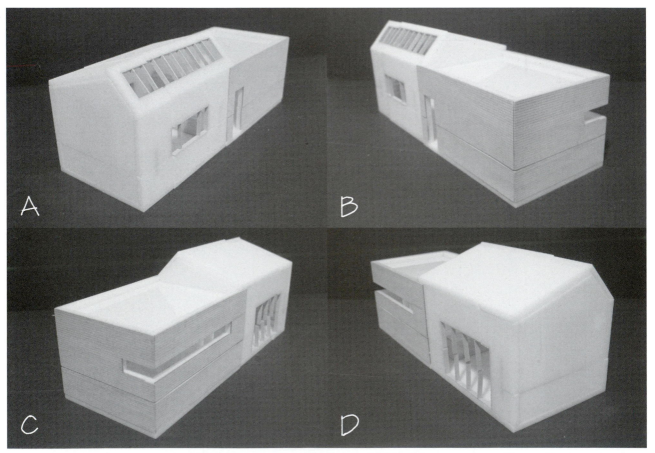

Each image shows the cabin rotated to expose a different corner and x, y, and z axes orientation used to create a paraline drawing, as referenced in the plan.

EXTERIOR ISOMETRIC

To draft an exterior isometric:

1. Establish the x, y, and z axes to begin the drawing. Using lightly drawn lines, your T-square, and your 30-60-90 triangle, draw a vertical line that represents the z axis at the bottom of a sheet of tracing paper. Add the x and y axes using your triangle, making sure they all meet at the exact same point.

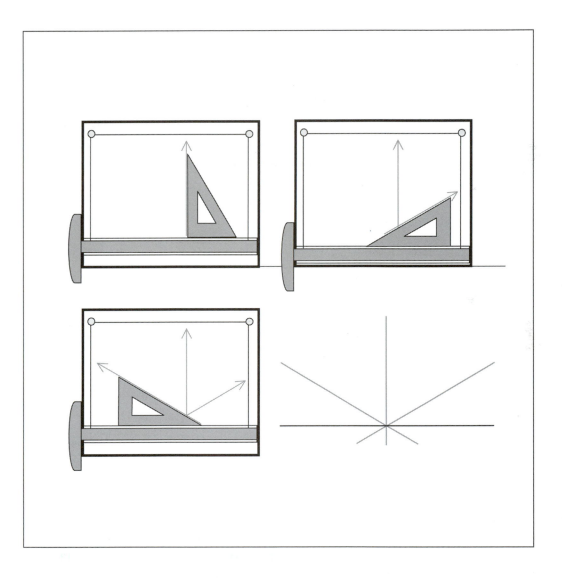

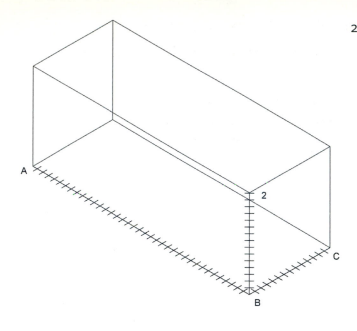

2. Using your scale, measure the largest overall length, width, and height of the entire space from the orthographic drawings (see Appendix) and create the basic rectangular form. Make sure to translate the dimensions measured from the orthographic drawings to the scale in which you are drawing the isometric. Note that whole feet are "ticked" off on the drawing steps; however, exact measurements will be marked with dots for clarity. Always use the true measurements when translating them to the isometric drawing.

- Every z-axis line is drawn vertically using the 90-degree side of the 30-60-90 triangle.

- Every x-axis and y-axis line is drawn using the 30-degree side of the 30-60-90 triangle.

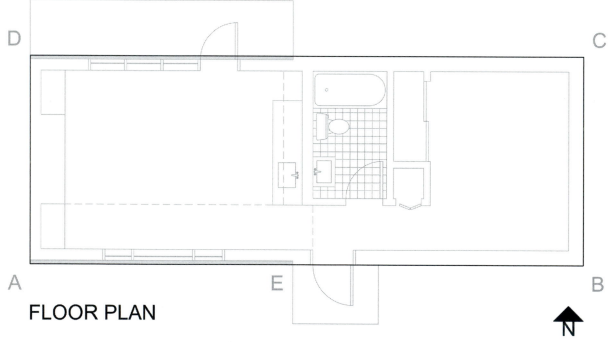

FLOOR PLAN

The shaded area indicates the 3" difference between the A–D length and the B–C length. This will be taken into account in the next step.

3. Subdivide the overall form with the major exterior architectural elements from the plan.

- Add the length, width, and height of these exterior elements to the isometric to create the overall skeleton of the building.

- Depending on the complexity of the structure, you may use multiple pieces of tracing paper to simplify this process. As you go, eliminate lines that are no longer necessary. This is done in the bottom drawing for clarity; however, you will still need some of the drawn-in guidelines to complete other steps.

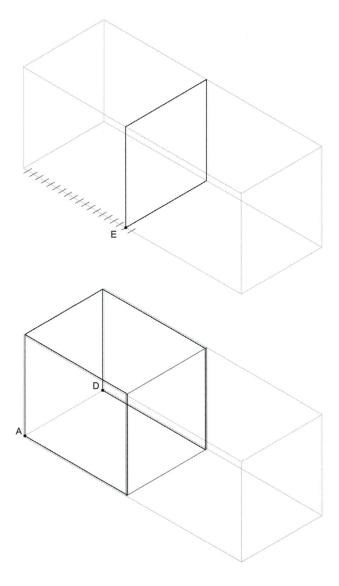

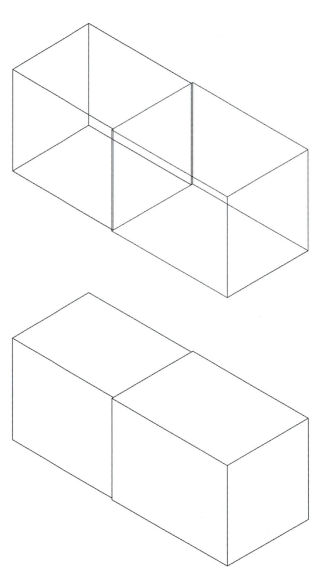

4. Add the major roof elements to the overall building. First, measure the roof plan on the orthographic drawings and translate the dimensions to the top of the building form in the isometric.

- The one-bedroom cabin has two major roof elements: the angled section and the flat section. Using your measurements from the orthographic drawings, create vertical planes at the locations where each roof section ends to indicate the edges.

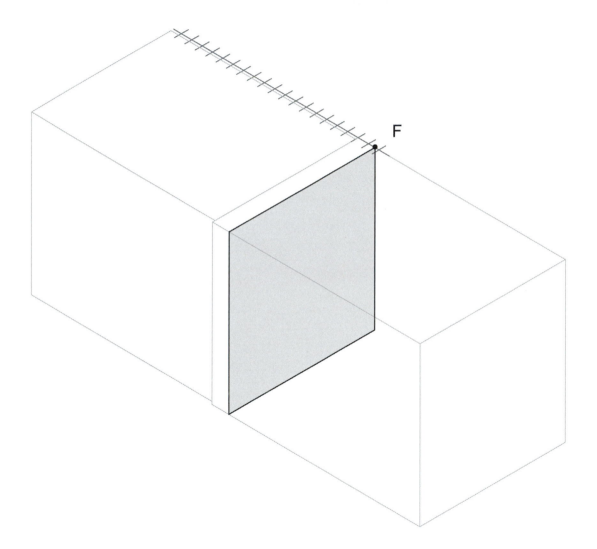

5. Next, add the heights of the exterior walls, which will dictate the roof heights and shapes. Create the walls' heights first, then pull the lines to the plane(s) created in step 4.

- In the case of this cabin, the angles of the sloped roof will not be 30, 45, 60, or 90 degrees, so you will have to use your adjustable triangle to complete them.

- Remember, angles will remain parallel once you have established them, so you can use the adjustable triangle once it is set each time you draw that parallel angle.

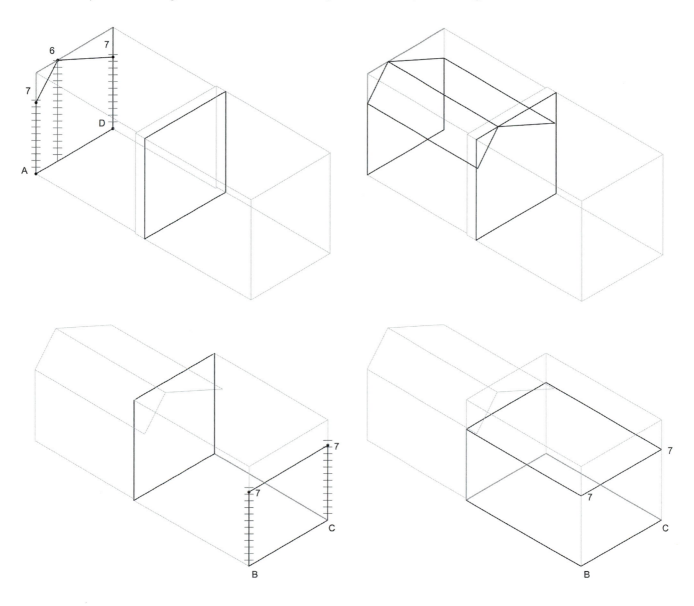

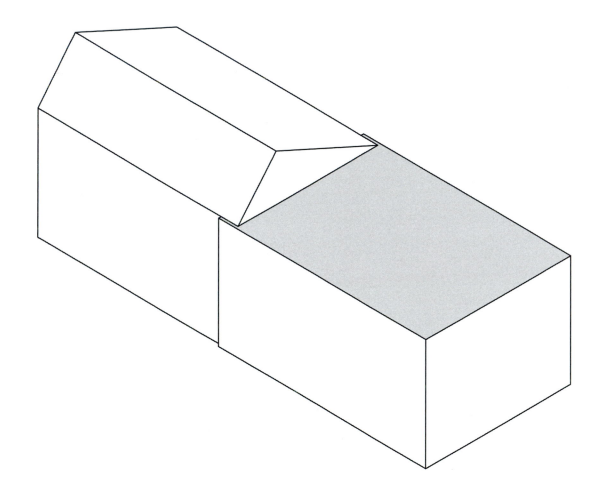

- Add any depth to the roof plane by measuring the roof plan and elevations.

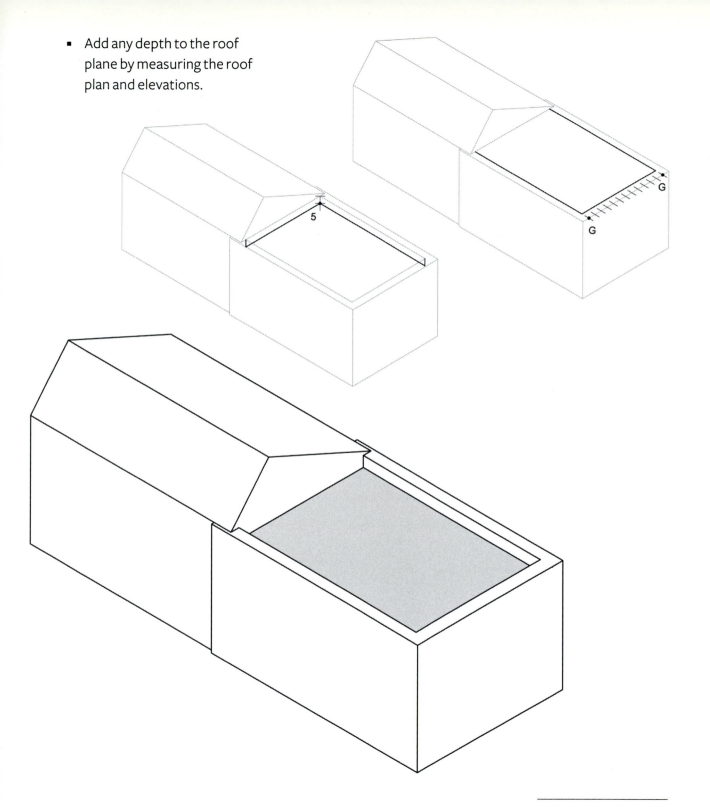

6. Finish adding all of the architectural elements, such as windows, skylights, and doors. Measure each element on the orthographic drawings and translate them to the isometric, just as in the previous steps.

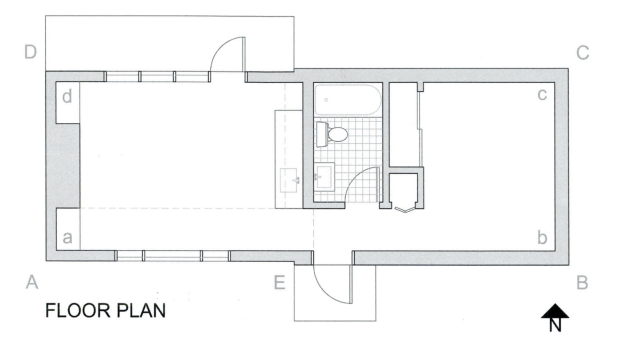

FLOOR PLAN

N

7. Finally, add depth and detail to the drawing, including finishes and trim work.

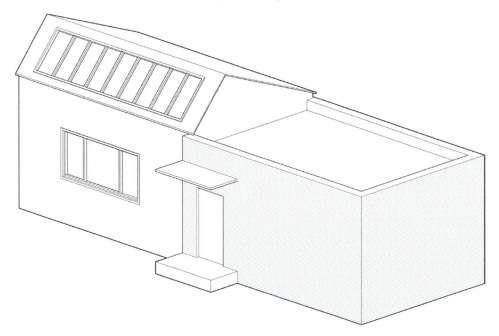

INTERIOR ISOMETRIC

To draft an interior isometric:

1. Determine what area you want to
    focus on for the interior isometric
    and "cut" the orthographic drawings
    at that point, using them to aid in the
    drawing of the isometric.

    - You can draw the entire floor
      plan or focus on just one
      portion of it. Since we created
      the entire building for the
      exterior isometric, a partial
      interior isometric of the
      fireplace will be created here.

    - For this drawing the floor
      plan is cut 4'-0" in front of the
      fireplace, as seen by the line
      with an arrowhead on the
      plan at right. That mark is a
      section line, and it indicates
      the location of the cut and
      the direction the viewer will
      be looking in the drawing. If
      the arrowhead pointed in the
      opposite direction, we would
      see the kitchen. This mark and
      others will be discussed in Book
      Four of the Studio Companion
      Series, *Presentation Basics.*

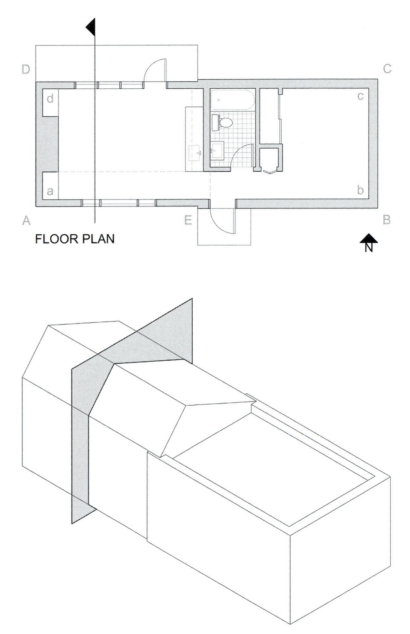

FLOOR PLAN

- Similarly to the exterior isometric, draw the x, y, and z axes and measure the overall length, width, and height of the interior space. This time, the 30-degree angles will be reversed around the horizontal line to create the interior corner.

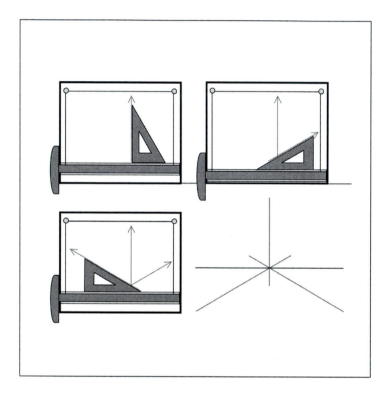

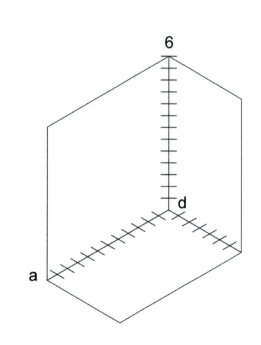

2. Subdivide the space, beginning with the major architectural and interior elements. Measure them on the orthographic drawings first, then draw them onto the isometric, using lightly drawn lines.

- The fireplace is located 3'-0" off the north and south walls. It is 1'-9" deep and 10'-0" tall.

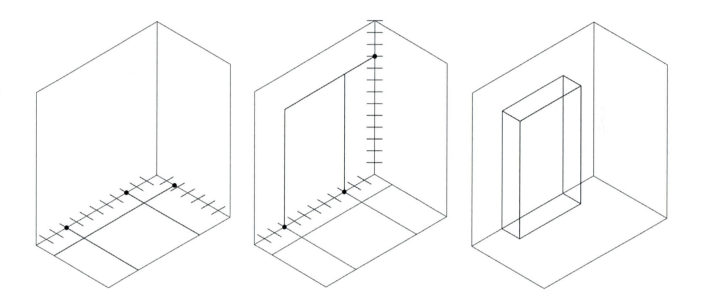

- The north and south walls are 10'-0" high, with a 13'-0" peak on the west wall located 3'-0" off the south wall. Since the dimensions are already marked on the drawing, it is easy to translate these architectural elements onto the isometric.

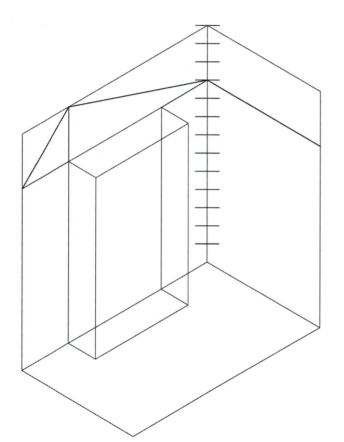
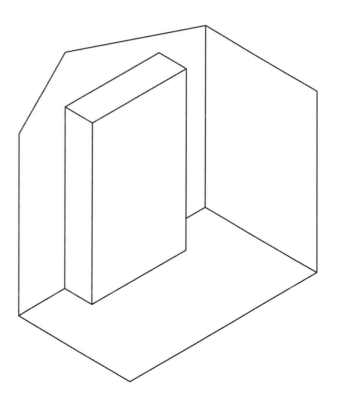

3. Using the same method as step 2, locate other items in the space, first marking them on the plan and then adding their heights.

- The built-in shelving has the same depth as the fireplace (1'-9"), so it has already been established on the isometric drawing. Simply add the heights and thickness to complete them. The tops of the shelves are located at 4'-0", 2'-8", and 1'-4" above the finished floor, respectively, and are each 2" thick.

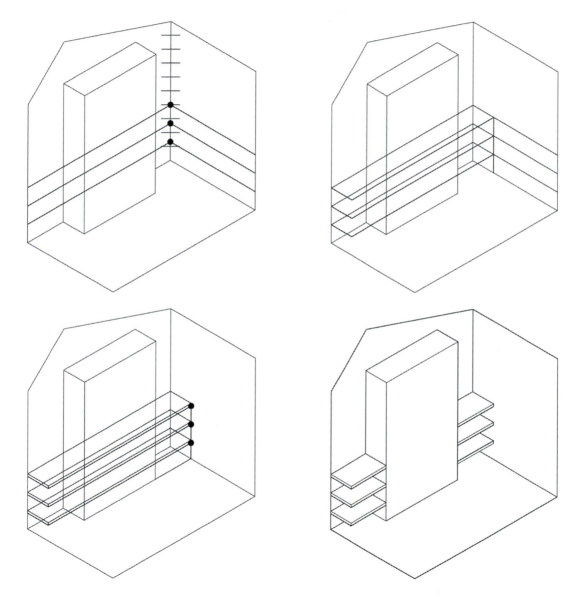

TIP: Remember that everything on the isometric is drawn to scale, so you can measure the thickness of the shelves on the "front edge" of the unit to make it easier to see.

4. Complete any details on the drawing, including trim work and finishes.

- The window is 2'-4" wide within a 9"-deep wall. The window trim is 2" on all sides, while the firebox trim is only 1½". The firebox itself is 1'-9" deep.

- The surface of the fireplace is made up of 3"-wide wood slats, and there is a 3"-wide wood baseboard on each of the walls.

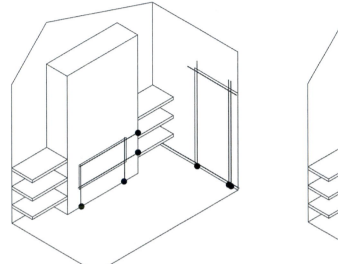
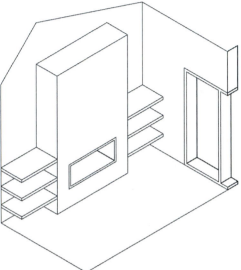

5. Finally, add line weights to the drawing to give it a more realistic feel.

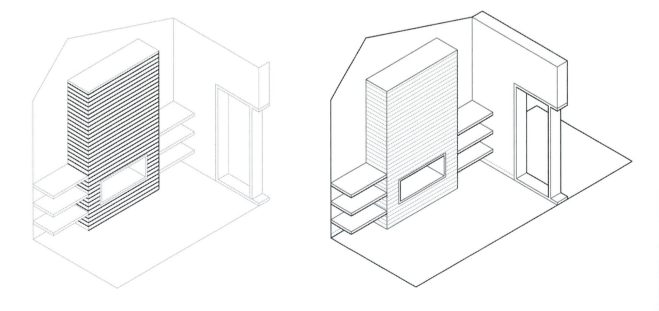

OBLIQUE DRAWINGS

There are two types of oblique drawings: plan oblique and elevation oblique.

A plan oblique rotates the drawing to view the planes at 45-degree or 30- and 60-degree angles, keeping the x and y axes at a 90-degree angle to each other. A plan oblique is unlike axonometric drawings, which use 120-degree angles for the x and y axes relationship. Remember, all items should be drawn to accurate scale.

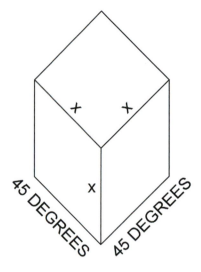 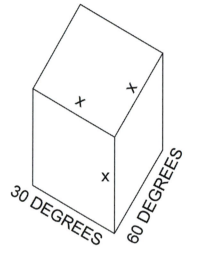 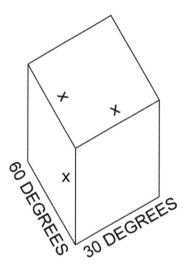

PLAN OBLIQUE OPTIONS

To create a plan oblique:

- Select which area of the orthographic drawing should be seen in the plan oblique.

- Determine the x, y, and z axes of the space you want to draw. Remember, the x and y axes will remain at a 90-degree angle to each other.

- Measure the orthographic drawings, specifically the elevations and sections, to acquire the heights needed to create the oblique drawing. You will not need to measure the basic floor plan because you will simply draw lines straight up from intersections on the floor plane.

To draft a plan oblique:

1. Establish the x, y, and z axes to begin the drawing.

    - This is much easier to do than it is in an axonometric drawing because you can simply tape down a copy of your floor plan at the angle you want to draw your plan oblique. For this example we will use a 45-degree angle.

    - Tape a piece of tracing paper over the floor plan, making sure to locate it so that it can accommodate the heights you will add to the drawing.

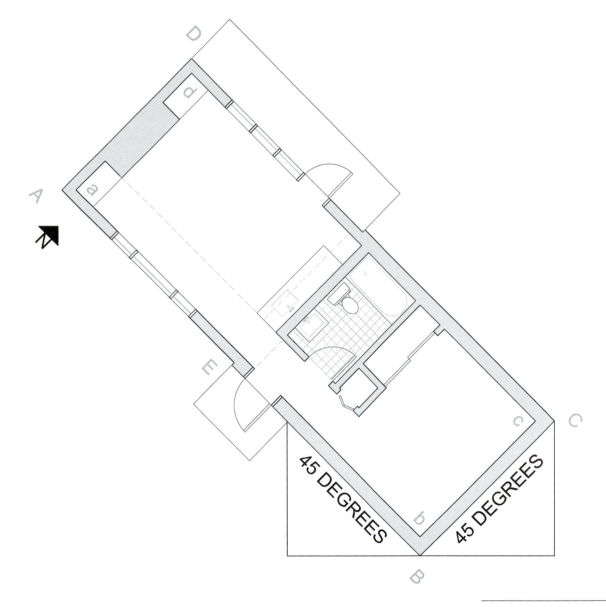

4. Complete any details, including the trim work and finishes.

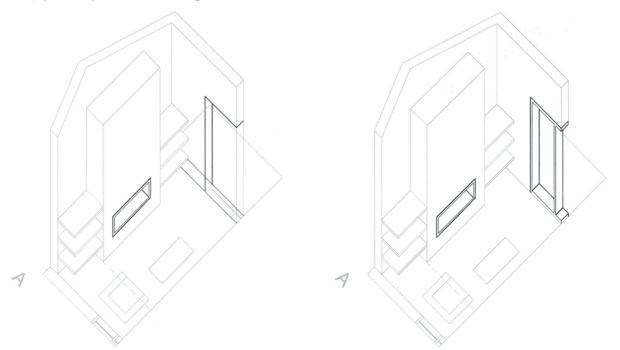

- Furniture can also be included in the drawing to assist someone in understanding the space.

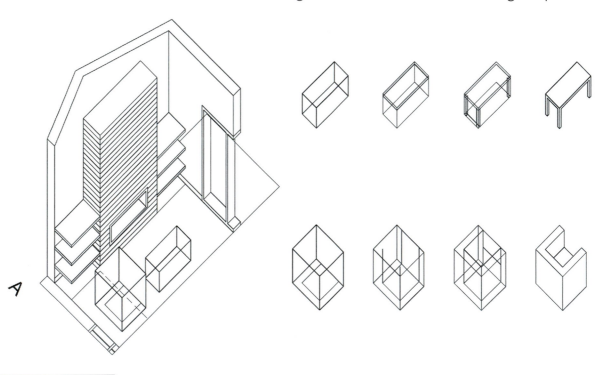

5. Add line weights to finish the drawing.

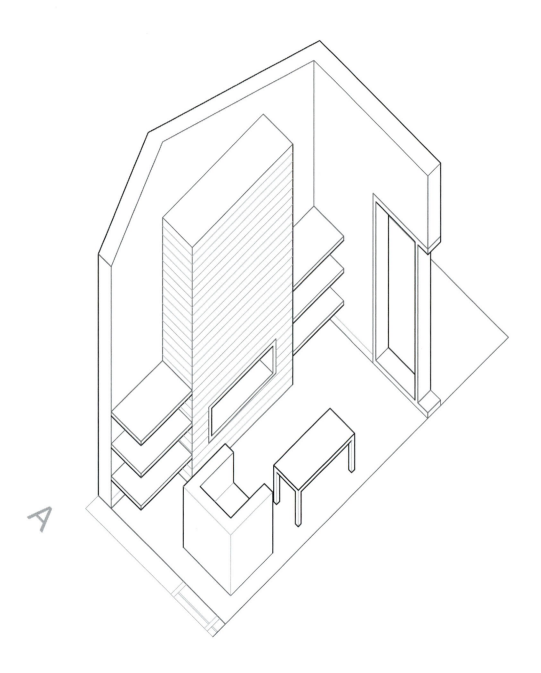

A

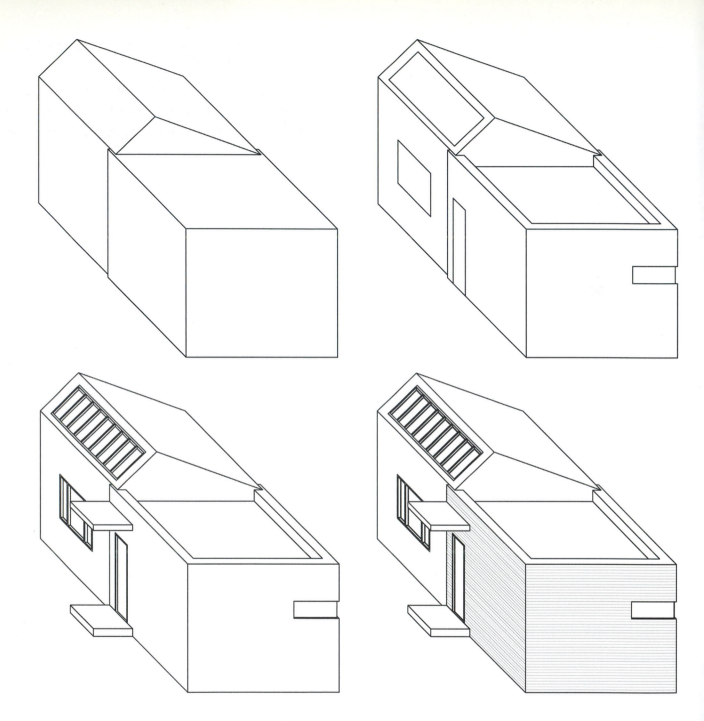

3. Follow the same steps that were used to create the isometric plan oblique, remembering to use the proper angle for parallel planes.

EXERCISE

|||||||||||||||||||||||||||||||||||||||||||||||||||||||||||||||||||||||||||||||||||||||||||||||||||||||||||||||||||||||||||||||||||||||||||||||||||||||

TOOLS NEEDED

Drafting board

Drafting brush

Drafting dots

Dry cleaning pad

Lead holder

Lead pointer

Leads

Scale

Tracing paper

Triangles

T-square

Set up your drafting area and prepare to draw a plan oblique.

1. Tape down the floor plan at the desired angle and highlight the area of the plan you want to see.
2. Tape down a large piece of tracing paper, using your T-square to line up the paper on the drafting board and use drafting dots to hold the paper in place on all four corners.
3. Place the T-square near the bottom of the page and prepare the x, y, and z axes to begin the plan oblique.
4. Using lightly drawn lines, create the corner of the plan oblique.
5. Follow the step-by-step directions from this chapter to complete the drawing of the one-bedroom cabin.

TIPS

- Make sure the T-square is "locked and loaded" against the drafting board and that your triangles ride firmly against the T-square.

- Remember that all lines along each axis are parallel as they relate to the original orthographic drawings.

- Layer multiple pieces of tracing paper to help clarify the drawing as you work.

EVALUATION

- Does the final drawing look like an extrusion of the floor plan? If not, review your tracing-paper layers to see if you can identify where you made a mistake, while reviewing the steps of the process.

- Are all of the lines parallel along their respective axes? If not, confirm which side of the triangle you used while drawing and make sure you were using your tools properly.

SUMMARY

Paraline drawings include three types of axonometric projection drawings and two types of oblique drawings. When drawn properly, they can communicate your design intent in the third dimension and help everyone to gain a better understanding of the space.

TWO

ONE-POINT PERSPECTIVE

OBJECTIVES

You will be able to identify and successfully create:

- One-point perspective drawings
- Scaled entourage, including people and objects

UNLIKE OTHER THREE-DIMENSIONAL DRAWINGS, A PERSPECTIVE DRAWING ALLOWS VIEWERS TO FEEL AS IF THEY ARE IN THE SPACE THEMSELVES. THESE THREE-DIMENSIONAL DRAWINGS CAN BE ONE-, TWO-, OR EVEN THREE-POINT PERSPECTIVES——WHICH MEANS THEY CAN HAVE ONE, TWO, OR THREE VANISHING POINTS.

In this chapter we will discuss how to draw one-point perspectives, as well as how to enhance them to be as realistic as possible through the use of entourage, which includes people, furniture, and other objects. There are many methods for creating a one-point perspective, but this chapter breaks down the process into simple and direct steps. It is meant as an introduction to perspective drawing, not an all-encompassing exploration of this skill.

ONE-POINT PERSPECTIVE

|||||||||||||||||||||||||||||||||||||||||||||||||||||||||||||||||||||||||||||||||||||||||||||||||

A one-point perspective is the simplest perspective to draw. It has only one vanishing point, so it is a direct look into a space. Just as with the paraline drawings in Chapter One, we will use the one-bedroom cabin so that you can see the difference between each of the three-dimensional drawings you have already encountered in this book.

A one-point perspective indicates:

- The size and shape of the space or object, including the overall length, width, and height as the viewer would see it while in the space.

- The relationship between people in the space and the space around them. This idea is referred to as the *human scale* of the space.

- All of the items that the designer wants the viewer to see. Like an isometric, a perspective can be drawn without a wall or plane so that the viewer can see inside the overall space more clearly.

CREATING A ONE-POINT PERSPECTIVE

To create a one-point perspective:

- Select which area should be dominant in the perspective and rotate the floor plan to visually assist with what you want to see.

- Measure the orthographic drawings and use those measurements to create the perspective drawing.

- Use a scaled floor plan to establish the critical elements needed to draw a perspective, listed below. This will be a new vocabulary for most students and will be defined, as well as illustrated, in the drafting portion of this chapter.

  - Picture plane (PP)

  - Station point or standing point (SP)

  - Cone of vision (COV)

- To start, draw a basic one-point perspective by creating the "back wall," called a picture plane, and locate the following items (again, all terms will be defined and illustrated in the next portion of this chapter).

  - Picture plane (PP)

  - Ground line (GL)

  - Horizon line (HL)

  - Vanishing point (VP)

  - Diagonal point (DP)

DRAFTING A ONE-POINT PERSPECTIVE

To draft a one-point perspective, you will need a scaled copy of the orthographic drawings (which can be written on), found in the Appendix at the back of the book, to reference as you create your perspective.

1. Determine what you would like to see from the floor plan in the perspective drawing.
2. Draw a horizontal line representing the **picture plane** (PP) at that location. In a one-point perspective, the picture plane must be parallel to the intended viewer in the space. In simple terms, the viewer's feet would be pointing squarely to the wall or area you want to draw.

    -   In a basic, rectilinear space like the one-bedroom cabin, the picture plane can be the rear fireplace wall.

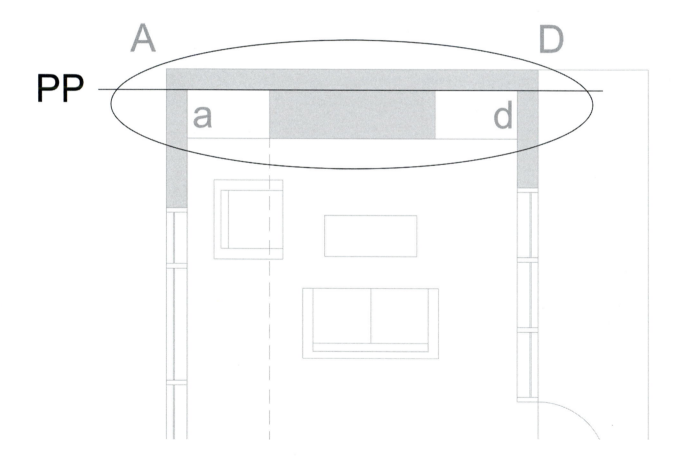

3. Establish your **station point** (SP), or the place where you want to stand to look at the space. I refer to this as the *standing point* to assist with that understanding. This, in tandem with the **cone of vision** (COV), will determine what you see in the perspective.

    - The cone of vision is a roughly 60-degree range in which you can see objects in the perspective drawing without distortion.

    - To see this more clearly, place the tip of the 60-degree portion of your 30-60-90 triangle at the station point and confirm that the cone of vision includes the area you want to see in the perspective. If the space isn't included, move the station point backward and forward, or side to side, until what you want to see is within the cone of vision. Remember to keep the viewer's toes pointing straight to the back wall, or picture plane.

    - Rarely would you locate the station point exactly in the middle of the space, widthwise. This will be too symmetrical and will not give you enough information about the space in your perspective.

    - You may have to locate the station point outside of the room or building in order to get the proper sight line. In that case, the "front" wall will not be drawn in the perspective.

    - Once this has been established, put the floor plan to the side as reference and prepare to draw the perspective.

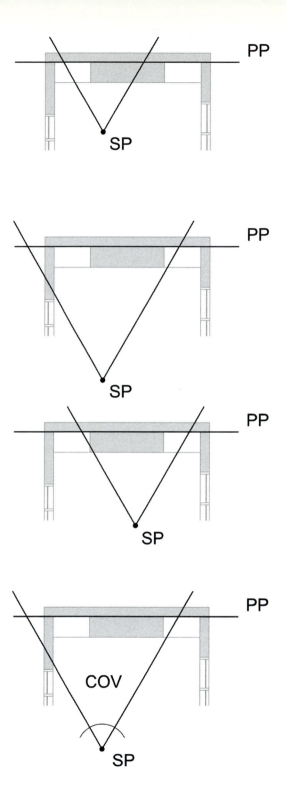

4. To start the perspective drawing, tape down a large piece of tracing paper onto the drafting board, using drafting dots on all four corners. With a scale, draw a rectangle in the center of the page the same width and height of the picture plane. The height of the picture plane equals the height of the room. The bottom line is known as the **ground line** (GL).

    - For our cabin, the width of the rectangle will be the distance between the corners labeled "a" and "d" on the floor plan. The height will be the distance from the ground line to the point labeled "6" on the west section.

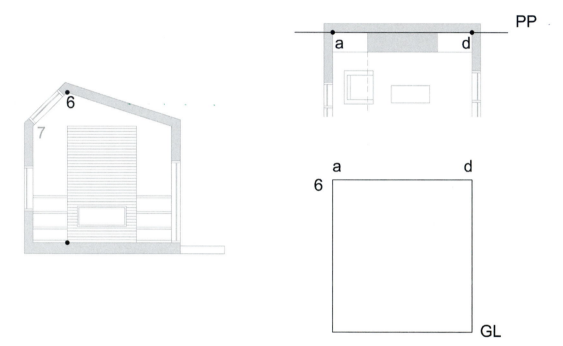

TIPS:

- Remember, the perspective may or may not be drawn at the same scale as the floor plan; perspectives are typically drawn at a larger scale.

    - It is easier to draw a perspective at a larger scale than you might eventually want for your presentation. You can use a copier to reduce the drawing to a size that will work later and then trace it.

5. Add a horizontal line 5'-0" above the ground line of the picture plane. This is known as the **horizon line** (HL), which is about the height of a typical viewer's eye.

TIP: If you were drawing the perspective from a child's vantage point, the horizon line would be lower. If you were drawing it from a second-story balcony, the line would be higher. In all cases, the horizon line should be at the viewer's eye line.

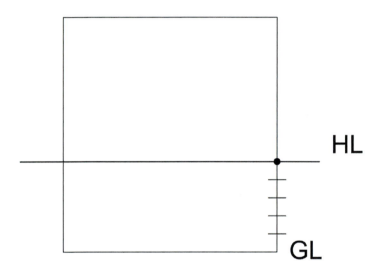

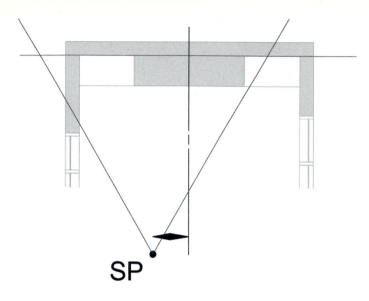

SP

6. Mark a **vanishing point** (VP) on the horizon line.

   ▪ The vanishing point is the location of the viewer looking onto the scene. It should be located along the line of sight from the station point established on the plan. The distance should be measured from the left or the right of the center of the plan and translated to the drawing at whatever scale you are using for the perspective.

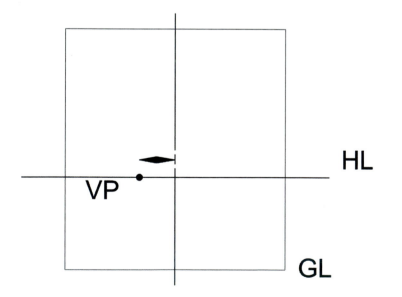

VP

HL

GL

7. Using your triangle, lightly draw lines from the vanishing point through the four corners of the picture plane. These are now the top two and bottom two corners of the room.

- This will be the first time you will not rest your triangle against your T-square, as the angle varies from corner to corner. Instead of "locking and loading" with the T-square, confirm that you are drawing the lines directly through the vanishing point and the exact corners of the picture plane. Failure to do so will negatively impact the rest of the drawing.

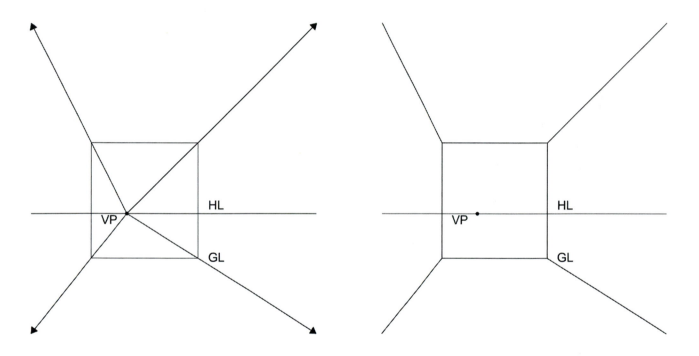

8. Establish the **diagonal point** (DP). Refer back to the floor plan to get the measurements needed to locate the diagonal point.

- At the scale of measurement in which the plan was created, measure the distance from the station point to the picture plane on the floor plan. This measurement will be translated to the perspective drawing to establish the diagonal point.

- Measuring from the vanishing point, locate the diagonal point along the horizon line on the same side of the vanishing point as the station point. Make sure to measure the distance at the scale in which the perspective is being drawn.

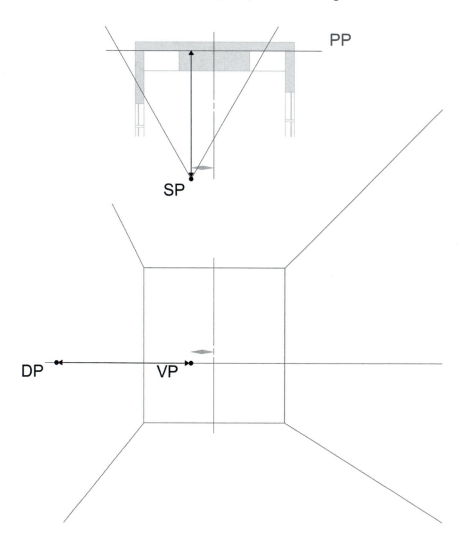

You now have a basic one-point-perspective skeleton of the room that you can use to locate objects in the space. These could include permanent architectural items, such as windows, fireplaces, and shelving units (like those in our one-bedroom cabin), or people and furniture, to make the space look more realistic.

The complexity and use of the following steps will vary depending on what you are drawing, but locating any item in the space will be done in a similar manner.

ONE-POINT-PERSPECTIVE DRAWING

Using the one-point-perspective drawing:

1. First, start with a new piece of tracing paper over the top of the basic drawing.

TIP: Remember to put drafting tape or drafting dots on all four corners of your tracing paper. You will be using a lot of tools and going in many directions over the top of the drawing, and you do not want it to rip.

2. Subdivide the space, beginning with the major architectural and interior elements. Measure them on the orthographic drawings and translate them onto the perspective, using lightly drawn lines.

    - Begin by establishing the overall room size. Reading the elevation drawing we know the north and south walls are 10'-10" so measure and mark them on each side.

    - Again from the elevation we know the peak of the wall is 13'-0", which was established when we drew the picture place.

        - The highest point of the west or fireplace wall was already established when the picture plane was drawn to determine its location. Use the dashed line on the floor plan and measure how far to the north the top of the ceiling is and then translate that dimension onto the perspective.

        - Draw the angle of the ceiling by connecting that point to the tops of the right and left walls using a triangle. Then, draw a line through the vanishing point and each new intersection of the walls and ceiling to create the ceiling plane.

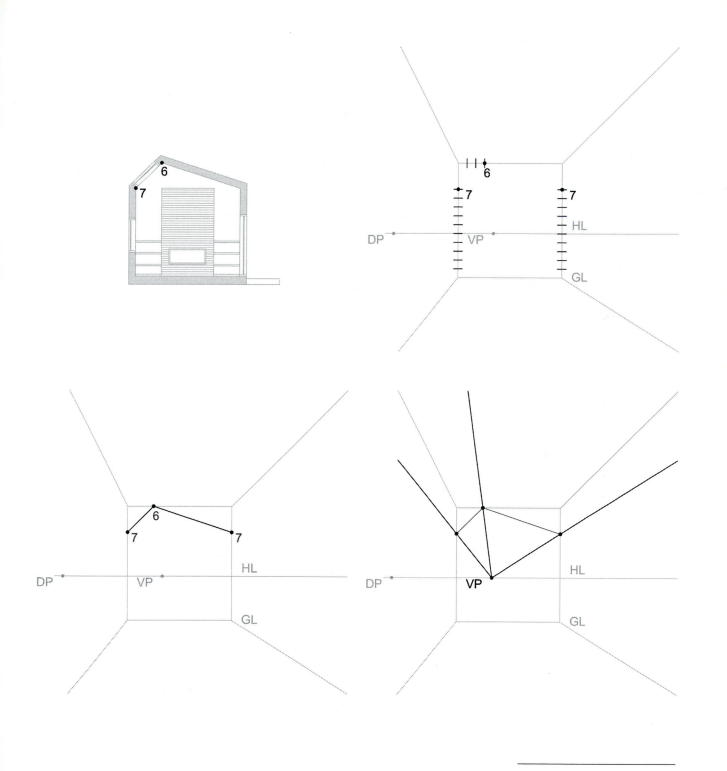

- Locate the width and depth of the fireplace and built-in shelving on the floor plane.
- Measure the depth of the fireplace on the floor plan and translate that dimension to the ground line, measuring out from the right or left wall.
  - The fireplace and shelves are only 1'-9" deep, so measure over 1'-9" from the left corner of the picture plane on the ground line.
  - Draw a line from the vanishing point through the 1'-9" measurement.
- Draw a line from the diagonal point corner on the floor plane. Where the two new lines intersect, draw a horizontal line, with your T-square "locked and loaded," across the floor plane. This is the depth of the fireplace and shelving.

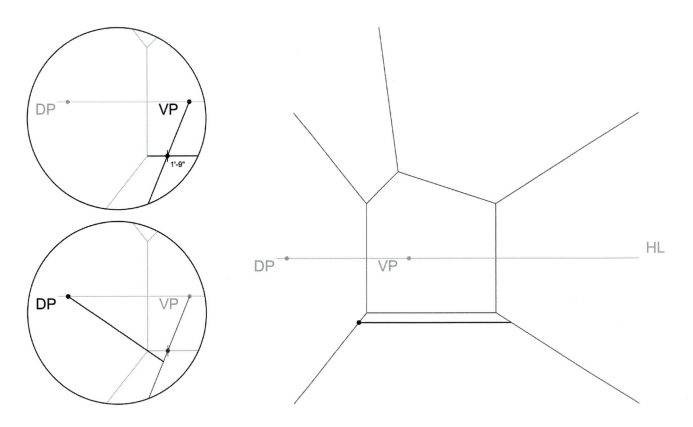

- Add the width of the fireplace to the floor plane by locating points 3'-0" from the north and south walls on the ground line. Then draw lines from the vanishing point, through these points, to the horizontal line that indicates the depth of the fireplace.

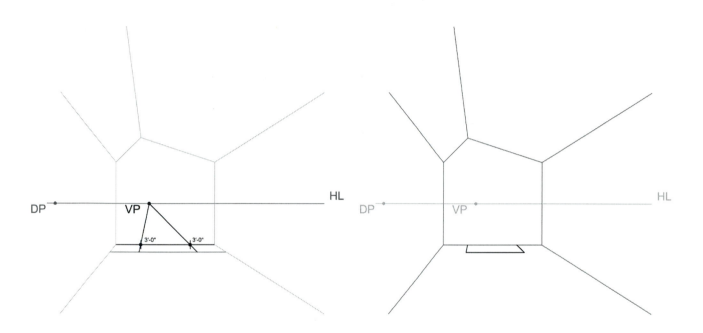

3. Add height and depth to create the overall skeleton of the elements.

- Using the 90-degree side of your triangle and your T-square, draw lines up from all four corners of the fireplace on the floor plane.
    - The fireplace is 10'-0" tall, so simply measure the height on the rear wall and then connect the overall shape of the fireplace by drawing a line from the measurement through the vanishing point.

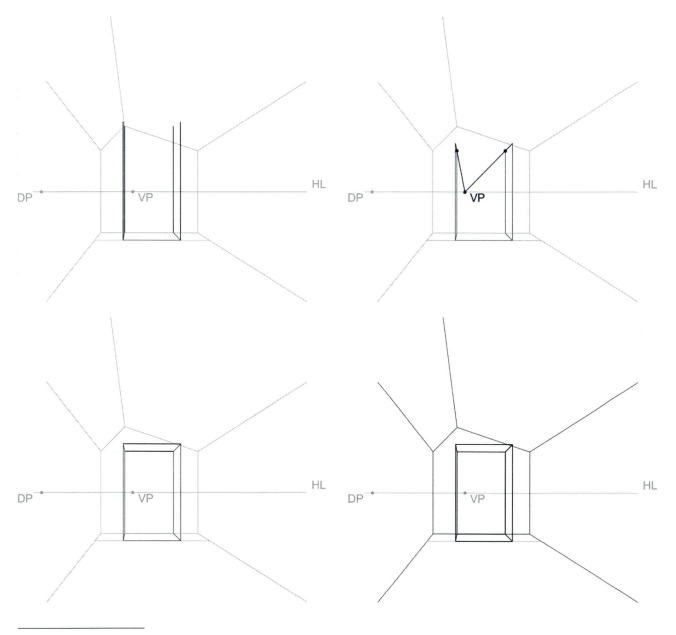

4. Add other built-in elements into the drawing.

- This includes the adjoining built-in shelving on both sides of the fireplace and the firebox itself.

- Translate the dimensions from the floor plan, just as in the previous steps. Using your scale of measurement, locate the heights of the shelves and firebox on the picture plan.

  - The tops of the shelves are located 1'-4", 2'-8", and 4'-0" above the floor.

  - Draw a horizontal line all the way across the picture plane and shelf depth to create the shelves on the right so you don't have to measure again.

  - The firebox is 1'-4" above the floor, 4'-0" wide, and 1'-9" tall.

  - Erase all the unneeded lines.

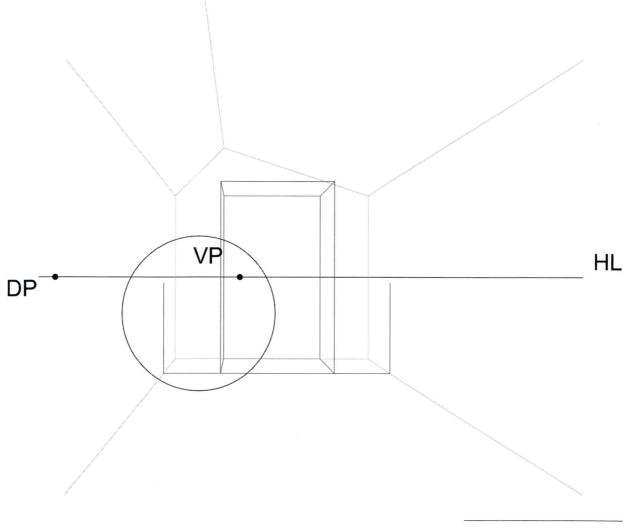

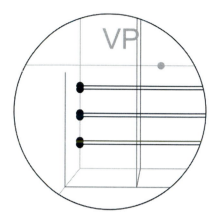
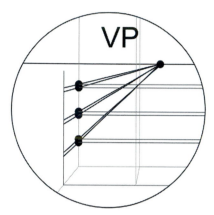
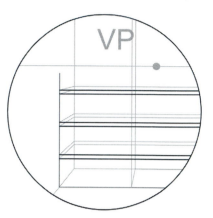

LEFT SIDE

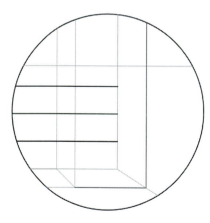
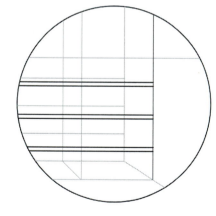
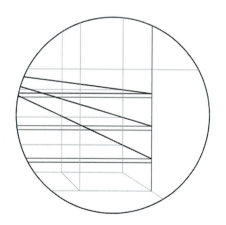

RIGHT SIDE

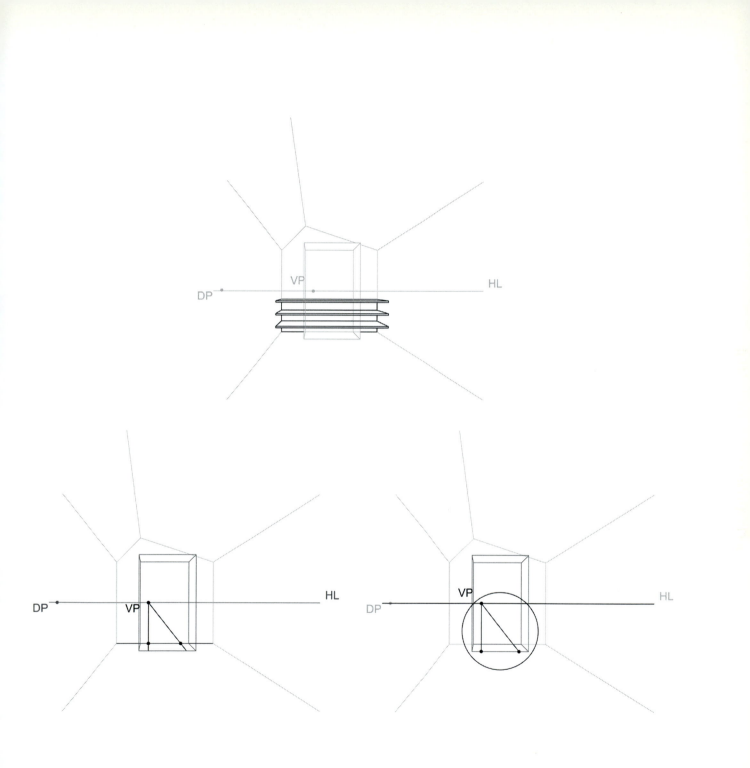

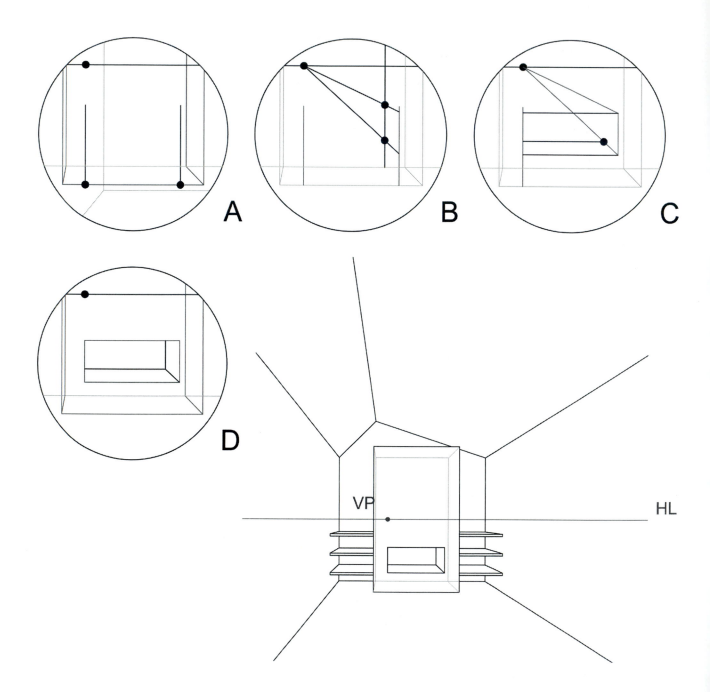

5. Finish adding the rest of the architectural elements, including windows, doors, and skylights. Measure each element from the paraline orthographic drawings and translate them to the perspective, just as in the previous steps.

- Measure the window height on the picture plane and draw a line through the measurement and the vanishing point onto the wall.

- Mark a point 4'-3" from the south wall on the ground line of the picture plane. This will be used to locate the distance to the edge of the window on the south wall.

- Draw a line from the vanishing point through the 4'-3" point on the ground line, extending it onto the perspective floor plane.

- Draw a line from the diagonal point through the lower left corner of the picture plane to the 4'-3" line on the floor plane.

- Using your T-square, draw a horizontal line to the south wall from the intersection of these two new lines. Then, using a 90-degree triangle, draw a vertical line on the south wall to create the edge of the window on the wall plane.

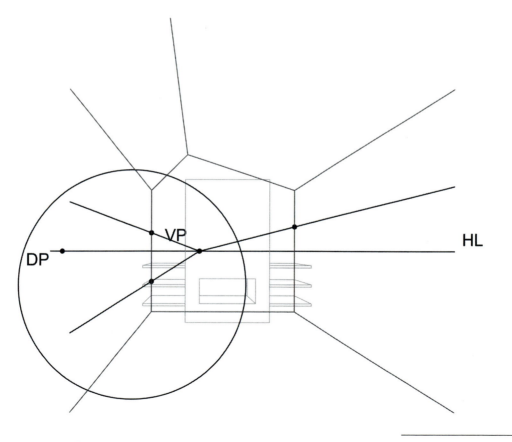

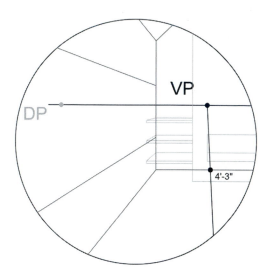
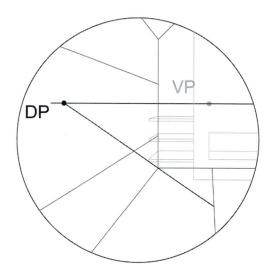

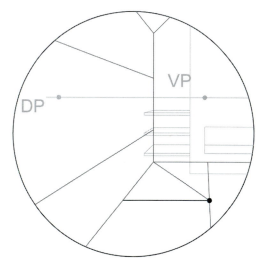
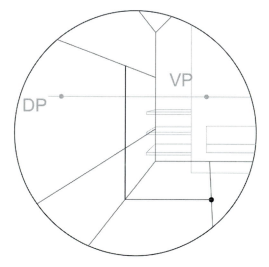

- Follow the same steps to create the window frame.

  - Measure 2" from the 4'-3" mark on the ground line of the picture plane.

  - Draw a line from the vanishing point through the new mark.

  - Draw a line from the diagonal point through the corner of the picture to the new line on the floor plane to ensure that you are getting the right width.

  - Draw a horizontal line with the T-square locked and loaded through the intersection to the south wall. Then, using a 90-degree triangle, draw a vertical line on the south wall to create the edge of the window trim.

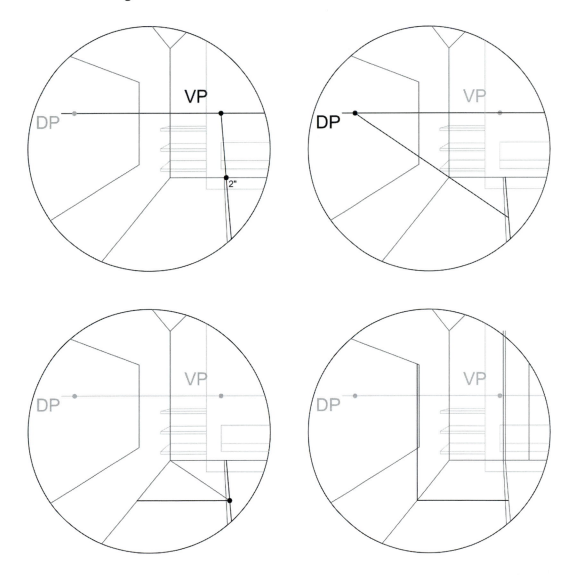

- Follow the same step to create the divisions of the window and its frame.

  - Measure 1'-0" from the 2" mark on the ground line of the picture plane.

  - Draw a line from the vanishing point through the new mark.

  - Draw a line from the diagonal point through the corner of the picture to the new line on the floor plane to ensure that you are getting the right width.

  - Draw a horizontal line with the T-square locked and loaded through the intersection to the south wall. Then, using a 90-degree triangle, draw a vertical line on the south wall to create the edge of the window.

  - Complete the 2" vertical window frame using the same steps.

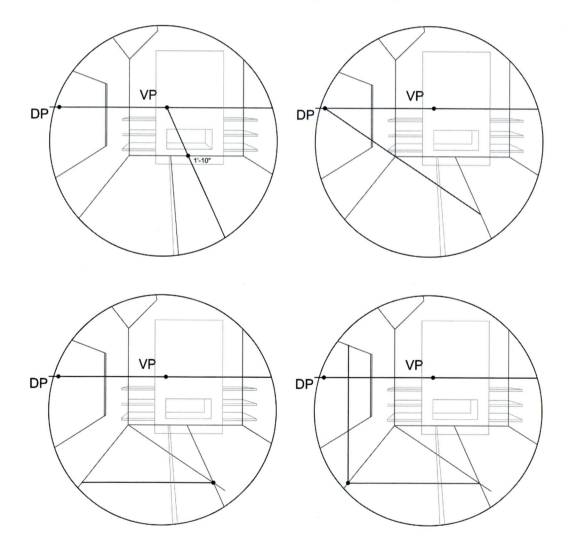

- Repeat these steps to locate the skylights on the south ceiling and the windows on the north wall.

TIP: To save time, mark all the dimensions of each skylight segment and trim all at once on the ground line.

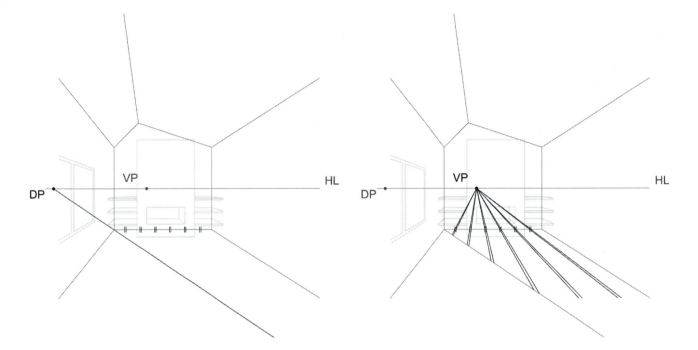

- Next, draw a line from the diagonal point through the corner of the picture plane. Then, draw the lines from the vanishing point through each point on the ground line. This will save a lot of confusion as you translate all of these measurements onto the floor plane, then the wall, and finally the ceiling plane.

- Draw a horizontal line with the T-square locked and loaded through all the intersections to the south wall. Then, using a 90-degree triangle, draw a vertical line on the south wall to create the edges of the skylights and the window trim.

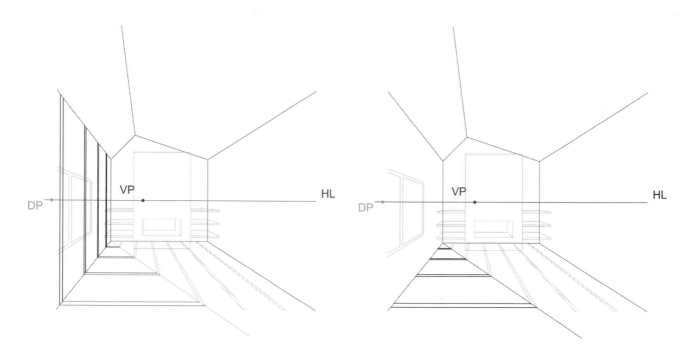

- Using your adjustable triangle and T-square, translate the lines from the wall to the ceiling plane. Remember the angle will be parallel with the angle of the line established on the back wall.

- Measure the section drawing to determine the height of the skylights and translate that onto the ceiling plane on the back wall of the perspective.

- Draw a line through the vanishing point and the new marks on the ceiling plane and trim accordingly.

- Finally, use the same steps to add the window to the north wall.

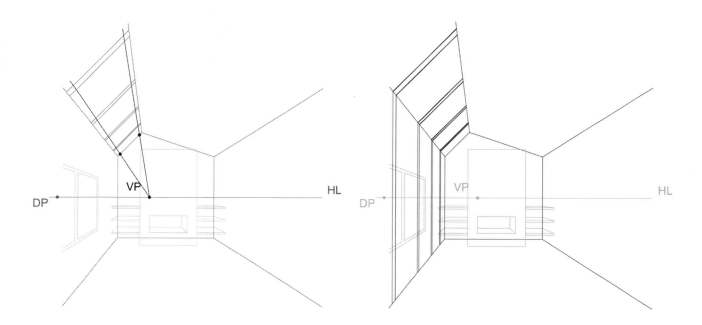

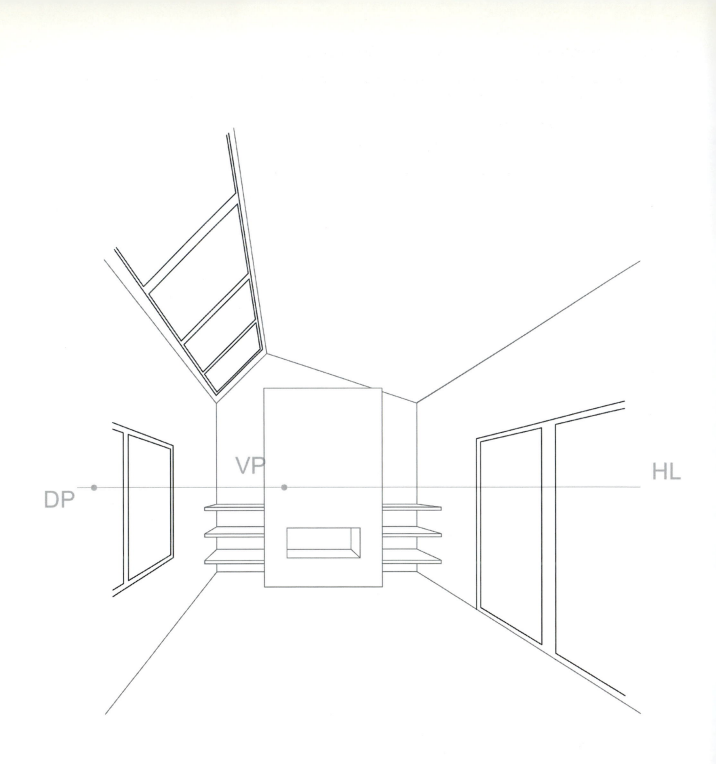

DP

VP

HL

6. Add depth and detail to the drawing, including finishes and trim work.

- To add depth to the window frames, extend the ground line beyond the original picture-plane width on both sides. Both walls are 9" deep; measure that distance on the extended ground line.

- Draw a line from the vanishing point through each 9" mark on the ground line, extending the floor width beyond the original perspective floor plane.

- Using your T-square, draw horizontal lines from the intersections left from when you located the window and trim on the floor of the wall plane to the new 9" line, creating the depth of the wall. Then, pull the lines up to the top of the window to complete the window trim.

- Using your 90-degree triangle, draw vertical lines to create the corners of the first and second window frames.

- Finally, measure and mark the height of the 2" trim on the wall of the picture plane. Draw a line through the vanishing points and these measurements and trim the windows accordingly.

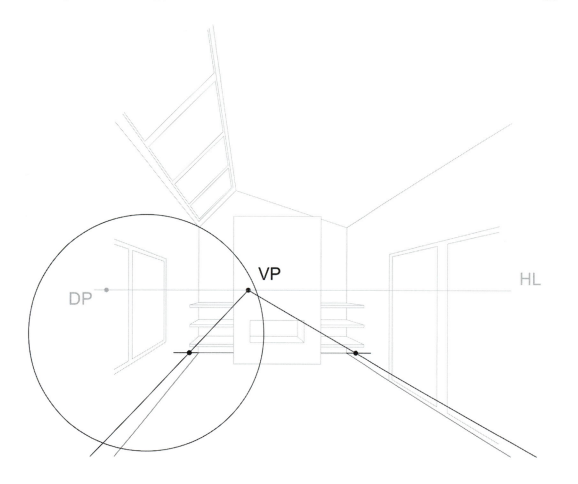

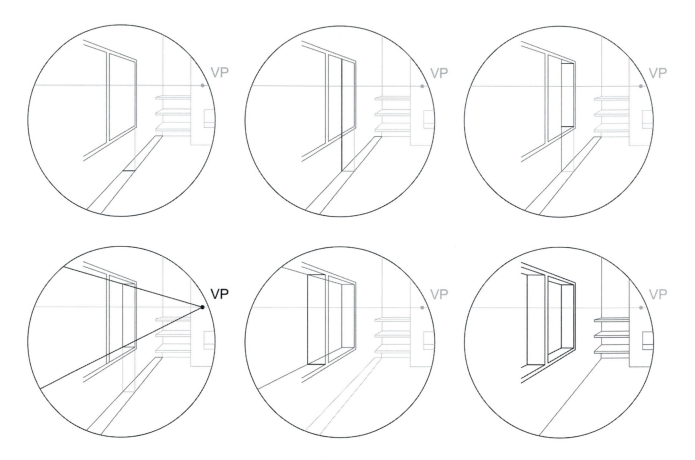

TIP: Notice that the depth of the second window frame is outside of the perspective grid. This is because of the distortion of the 60-degree cone of vision, so there is no reason to draw it.

- Repeat these steps to locate the depths of the skylights.

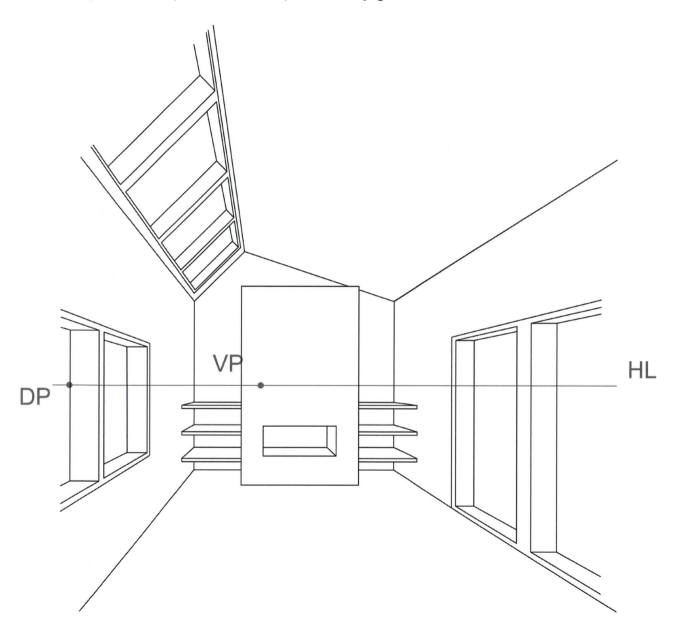

DP

VP

HL

- Add the 3" wood slats to the fireplace, the 1½" trim around the firebox, and the 3" baseboard to the walls in a similar fashion.

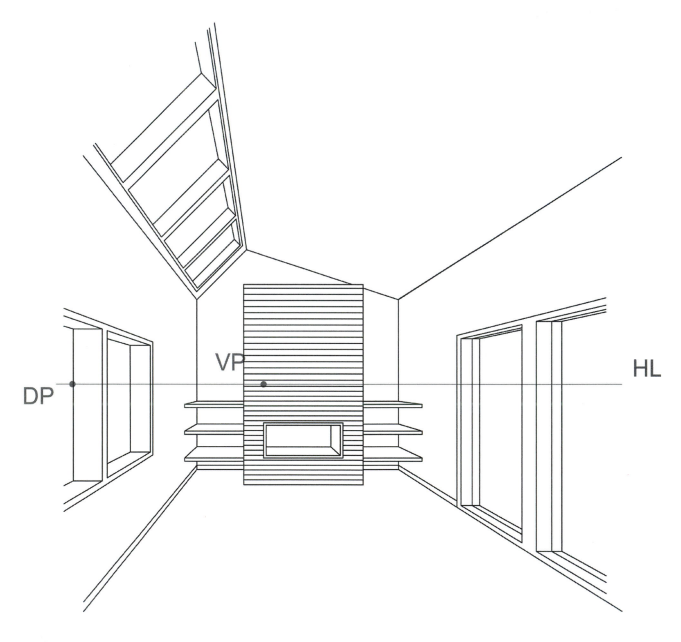

7. Finally, add the furniture and people into the space. This is known as *entourage*, and it enhances the drawing to make it feel more realistic. Just as stated earlier, a separate piece of tracing paper can be used to make the process simpler.

- First, locate the furniture on the floor plane. The chair is located 3'-3" off the picture plane and 1'-0" from the south wall. The chair itself is 2'-6" deep, 2'-10" wide, and 2'-6" tall, with a seat 1'-3" off the ground. The arms and back are 6" wide.

  - Begin with the width distances first, then add the length distances for clarity on the ground line, then the floor plane.

  - Add the heights to the furniture. At this angle in our perspective you will not be able to see the seat of the chair so there is no reason to add it to the drawing.

  - Add the table using the same steps.

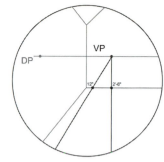

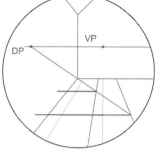

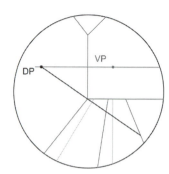

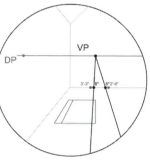

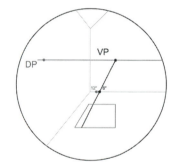

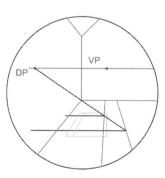

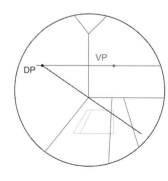

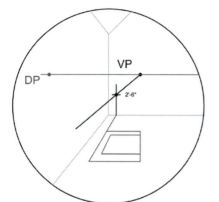
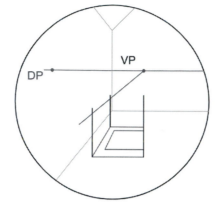
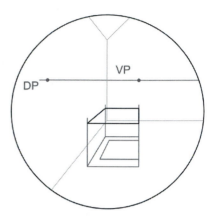
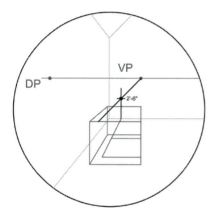
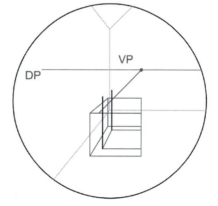
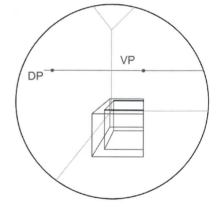

- Locate people in the perspective. Remember to put a person's "eyes" on the horizon line. That way, the viewer gains an understanding of the space as it relates to a human—referred to as *human scale*. Without people in the drawing as a reference, the space may not seem as realistic as it could.

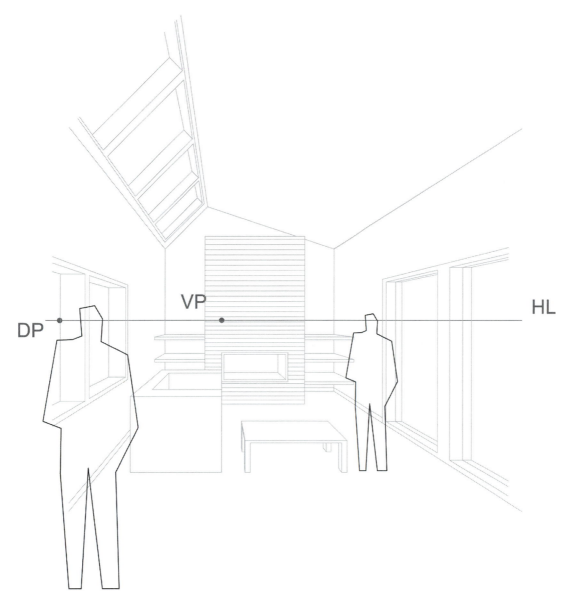

DP

VP

HL

TIP: You can find people and other entourage, like plants and toys, in books dedicated to the subject, or simply trace people from photographs or magazines.

To truly finish the perspective drawing, you should trace it one last time and add line weights. Refer to Chapter Two in *Drafting Basics,* Book Two of the Studio Companion Series, to review line weights.

You can increase or decrease the size of your final drawing using a copier, allowing you to customize the size to fit your presentation.

ADDING ROUND OBJECTS

As you progress and your design becomes more complicated, you can add curved or rounded items to your designs. For example, a simple round ottoman could be added in front of the chair instead of a small coffee table.

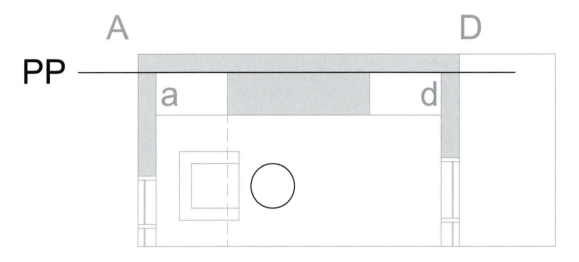

- First, locate the round shape on the floor plane as a square, just as you did with the other objects in the drawing. Then add the height to the square to make it a three-dimensional rectilinear form.

- Next, subdivide the top square by creating lines from the corners and vanishing point, and keep subdividing until you have enough tangential points to complete the circle. Use an oval template, French curve, or flexible curve to draw the top of the round ottoman.

- The ottoman is centered 6" in front of the chair and is 1'-10" round and 1'-3" tall. The overall chair was 2'-10" but if you subtract the two widths of the arms (6" each) that means the seat width is 1'-10", the width of the ottoman. If this were not the case you would simply measure the width of the ottoman on the ground line of the picture plane just as in previous steps.

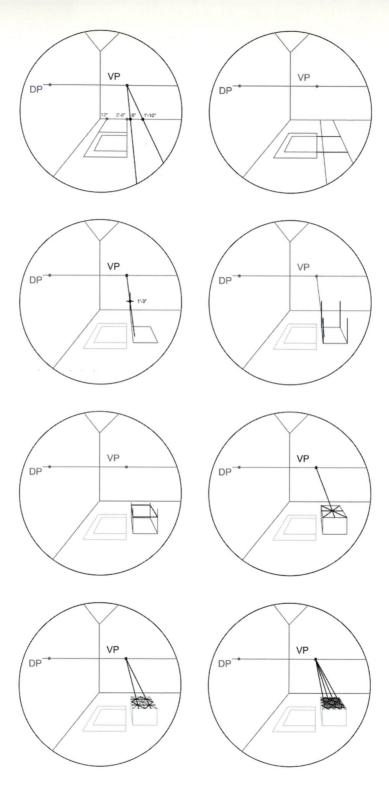

EXERCISE

|||||||||||||||||||||||||||||||||||||||||||||||||||||||||||||||||||||||||||||||||||||||||||||||||||||||||||||

TOOLS NEEDED

Drafting board

Drafting brush

Drafting dots

Dry cleaning pad

Lead holder

Lead pointer

Leads

Scale

Tracing paper

Triangles

T-square

Set up your drafting area and prepare to draw a one-point perspective of the kitchen in the one-bedroom cabin.

1. Tape down a large piece of tracing paper, using your T-square to line up the paper on the drafting board.

2. Use drafting dots to hold the paper in place on all four corners.

3. Take a copy of the floor plan and evaluate it to determine what you want to see in the perspective, locating the following:

    - Picture plane (PP)

    - Station point or standing point (SP)

    - Cone of vision (COV)

4. Draw the picture plane as explained in this chapter and note the following:

    - Picture plane (PP)

    - Ground line (GL)

    - Horizon line (HL)

    - Vanishing point (VP)

    - Diagonal point (DP)

5. Using lightly drawn lines, create the perspective for the overall room.

6. Follow the step-by-step directions to complete the drawing of the kitchen in the one-bedroom cabin.

TIPS

- Accuracy is the most important thing in drawing a perspective.

  - Make sure your lines extend from the vanishing point through the corners of the drawing, carefully creating the floor, walls, and ceiling.

- Use multiple pieces of tracing paper to help clarify the drawing as you work, and keep the sheets so that you can review them if you find a mistake later.

- Use different colored pencils to assist with understanding and differentiating what is a floor, a wall, a ceiling, or a line of measurement.

- Use different colored highlighters on a copy of the perspective to determine line weights before you do the final drawing.

EVALUATION

- Does the final drawing appear to be square and true? If not, review your tracing-paper layers to see if you can identify where you made a mistake, while reviewing the steps of the process again.

- Does each element within the perspective appear to be parallel or equal in proportion to the paraline drawings? If not, again review your tracing papers to see if you can determine where the drawing went wrong.

- Ask a fellow student to review your work, or look at the drawing upside down to see if you can spot a mistake. Sometimes it just takes an extra set of eyes to identify an error.

SUMMARY

One-point perspectives are a great way to gain an inside understanding of a space because they use human scale in their creation. Drawing one-point perspectives is a tough skill to learn, but with practice you will get better and faster.

THREE

TWO-POINT PERSPECTIVE

OBJECTIVES

You will be able to identify and successfully create:

- Two-point perspective drawings
- Scaled entourage, including people and objects

THIS CHAPTER WILL DISCUSS HOW TO DRAW TWO-POINT PERSPECTIVES, AS WELL AS HOW TO ENHANCE THEM TO BE AS REALISTIC AS POSSIBLE THROUGH THE USE OF ENTOURAGE, WHICH INCLUDES PEOPLE AND FURNITURE. JUST LIKE A ONE-POINT PERSPECTIVE, THERE ARE MANY METHODS TO CREATE A TWO-POINT PERSPECTIVE, BUT THIS CHAPTER BREAKS DOWN THE PROCESS INTO SIMPLE AND DIRECT STEPS. AGAIN, THIS TEXT IS INTENDED AS AN INTRODUCTION TO PERSPECTIVE DRAWING AND NOT AN ALL-ENCOMPASSING EXPLORATION OF THIS SKILL.

TWO-POINT PERSPECTIVE

A two-point perspective is more complicated to draw than a one-point perspective because it has two vanishing points, as the name indicates, but the basic ideas remain the same. The additional vanishing point allows for a more realistic view of the space. We will continue to use the one-bedroom cabin so that you can see the difference between each of the three-dimensional drawings you have already encountered in this book.

A two-point perspective indicates:

- The size and shape of the space or object, including the overall length, width, and height as the viewer would see it while in the space.

- The relationship between a person in the space and the space around them, referred to as *human scale*.

- All of the items that the designer wants the viewer to see. As with the other drawings in this book, a perspective can be drawn without a wall or plane so that the viewer can see inside the overall space more clearly.

CREATING A TWO-POINT PERSPECTIVE

To create a two-point perspective:

- Select which area should be dominant in the perspective drawing and rotate the floor plan to visually assist with what you want to see.

- Measure the orthographic drawings and use those measurements to create the perspective drawing.

- Use a scaled floor plan to establish the critical elements needed to draw a perspective, listed below. Some of these terms you learned in the previous chapter, but others will be new vocabulary, which will be defined and illustrated in the drafting portion of this chapter.

  - Picture plane (PP)

  - Station point or standing point (SP)

  - Central axis of vision (CAV)

  - Vanishing points (VP), both left and right

  - Measuring points (MP), both left and right

  - Cone of vision (COV)

- To start, draw a basic two-point perspective by creating the picture plane and locate the following items. Again, the new terms will be defined and illustrated in the next portion of this chapter.

  - Picture plane (PP)
  - Ground line (GL)
  - Horizon line (HL)
  - Vertical measuring line (VML)
  - Vanishing points (VP)
  - Measuring points (MP)

DRAFTING A TWO-POINT PERSPECTIVE

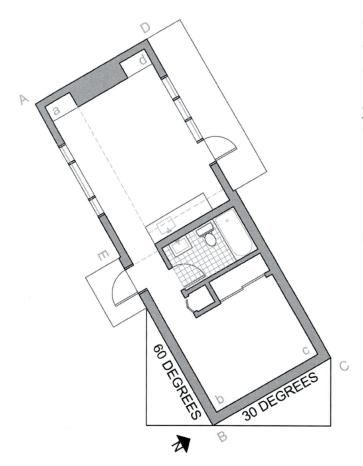

To draft a two-point-perspective grid, you will need a scaled copy of the floor plan and elevation or section that can be written on (see Appendix), to reference as you create your perspective.

1. Determine what you would like to see from the floor plan in the perspective.

    - The fireplace wall will continue to be the focus of our drawings.

2. Tape a copy of your floor plan onto your drafting board at all four corners, rotating it to view the front planes of the cabin at 30- and 60-degree angles. Then, tape a large piece of tracing paper over the top of your floor plan.

    - The angles can vary depending on what you want to see in the space, but they will always remain parallel from the floor plan to the perspective drawing.

3. Establish a **picture plane** (PP) by lightly drawing a horizontal line on the tracing paper, using your T-square and lead holder.

- In the case of the one-bedroom cabin, draw the picture plane through the front corner of the shelving (to the left of the fireplace by point "a").

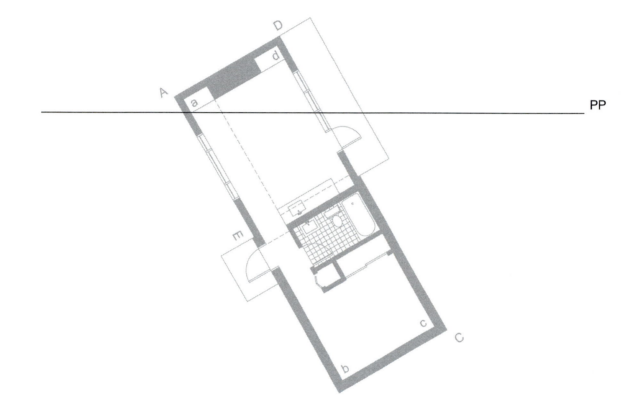

4. Establish your **station point** (or *standing point*) (SP), or where you want to stand to look at the space. This, in tandem with the **cone of vision** (COV), will determine what you see in the perspective.

- Use the point of the 60-degree portion of your 30-60-90 triangle as the station point and the angle as the cone of vision to assist in understanding the best location to take the perspective.

- Move your triangle closer to or farther away from the picture plane, or left to right, until what you want to see is within the cone of vision.

- Once you have determined the best station point, mark it on the tracing paper.

- Remember to keep the viewer's toes pointing straight at (parallel to) the picture plane.

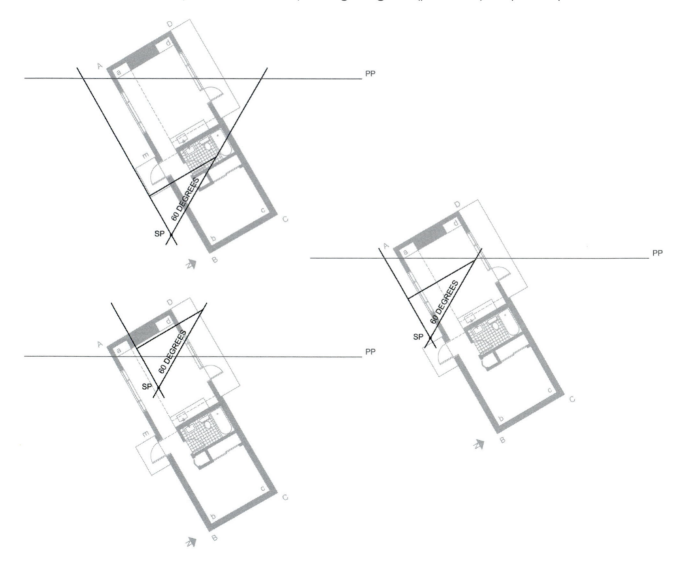

5. Draw a vertical line from the station point to the picture plane, creating the **central axis of vision** (CAV).
6. Establish the **vanishing points** (VP) on the right and left sides.
   - Draw a line perpendicular to each wall on the floor plan through the station point to intersect the picture plane, using your 30- and 60-degree triangle respectively. These angles will change if you change the angles in step 2.
   - Label the points where the lines intersect the picture plane as the **right vanishing point** (RVP) and the **left vanishing point** (LVP).

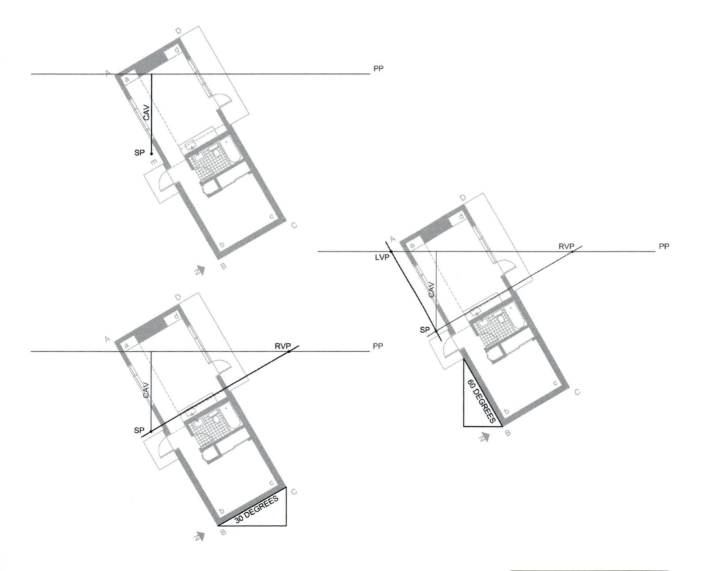

7. Establish the **measuring points** (MP) on the right and left sides.

- Rotate the radius from the right vanishing point to the station point until it intersects the picture plane, marking the **left measuring point** (LMP).

- Repeat this step at the left vanishing point to mark the **right measuring point** (RMP).

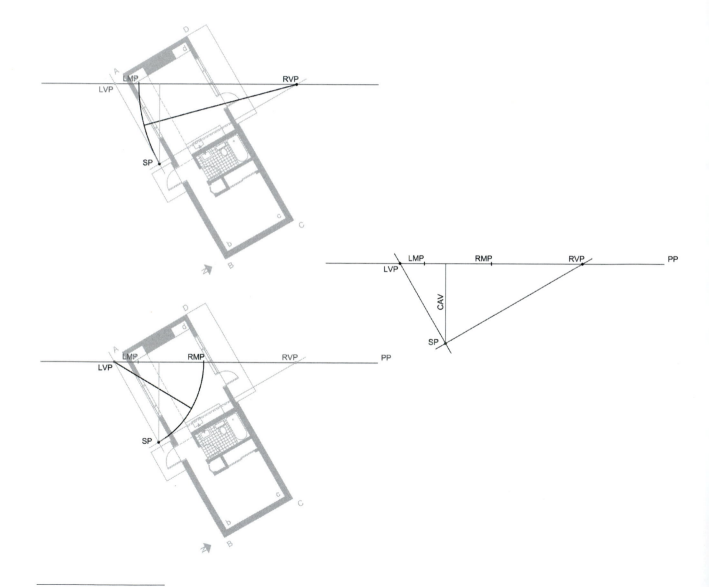

8. At the scale used to draw the floor plan, measure the distance along the picture plane from the central axis of vision to the left and right measuring points and document the dimensions in feet and inches.

9. Similarly, measure the distance from the central axis of vision to the left and right vanishing points and document the dimensions in feet and inches.

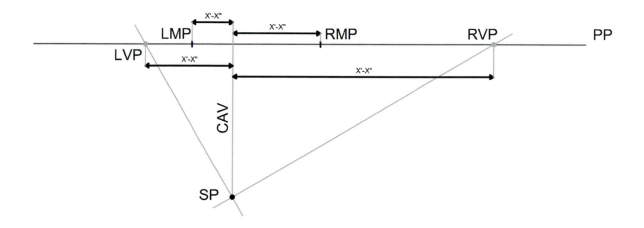

10. Remove the tracing paper and floor plan from the drafting board, keeping the information to the side to use as a reference in the next steps. This information will be referred to as the *measurement document*.

11. Tape down a new, large sheet of tracing paper and begin the perspective by drawing a **ground line** (GL) close to the bottom of the page. Label it "GL."

12. Establish the **vertical measuring line** (VML) by drawing a perpendicular line to the ground line, using your T-square and the 90-degree side of your triangle.

- The location of the vertical measuring line can vary along the ground line. Look at the measurement document for a hint at where to locate it. Which pair of vanishing and measuring points, the left or right, is closest to the central axis of vision?

    - In our case, the left pair is closer. This means that the perspective drawing will most likely be more dominant on the right side. Locate the vertical measuring line to the left of the center of the page.

    - Beginning at the ground line, tick the unit of measure of your space along the vertical measuring line and the ground line, at the scale you selected for the perspective drawing.

        - Our floor plan measures 12'-0" wide (in the east–west direction) by 18'-0" long (in the north–south direction) for the living-room/kitchen area only. We know that the 18'-0" length is greater than what we will see in the 60-degree cone of vision, so we will use 14'-0" instead.

        - The highest ceiling point in the space is at 13'-0", with the side walls measuring 10'-0" high, as seen on the elevation and section drawings.

    - Use these dimensions to mark the measurements on the vertical measuring line and the ground line.

    - Draw a line across the entire sheet at the 5'-0" high mark to create the horizon line.

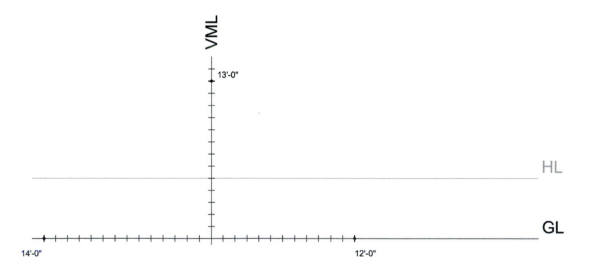

13. Transfer the two vanishing points and two measuring points to the **horizon line** (HL) on this drawing and label them properly.

- Remember to adjust the scale of your measurements accordingly to the scale used for the perspective drawing, not the floor plan.

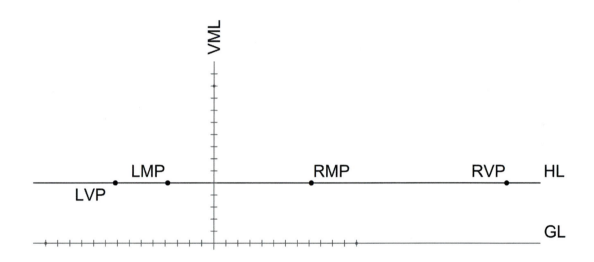

14. Draw a line from each of the vanishing points to the intersection of the ground line and the vertical measuring line. This is the front corner of the perspective drawing

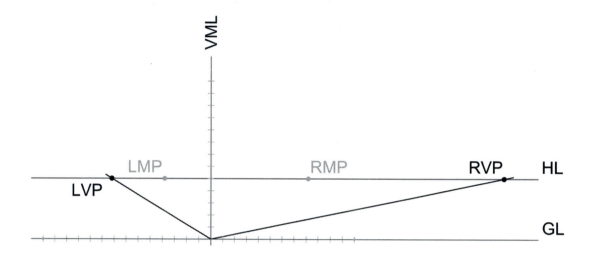

15. Create the overall floor plane. Draw it to the largest rectangular dimension needed for the space.

- Draw lines from the measuring points to the tick marks on the ground line that indicate the lengths of the east–west and north–south walls. To create the line for the 12'-0" east–west wall, draw a line from the left measuring point, through the vertical measuring line, to the 12'-0" tick mark on the ground line. To create the 14'-0" north–south wall, draw a line from the right measuring point, through the vertical measuring line, to the 14'-0" tick mark on the ground line.

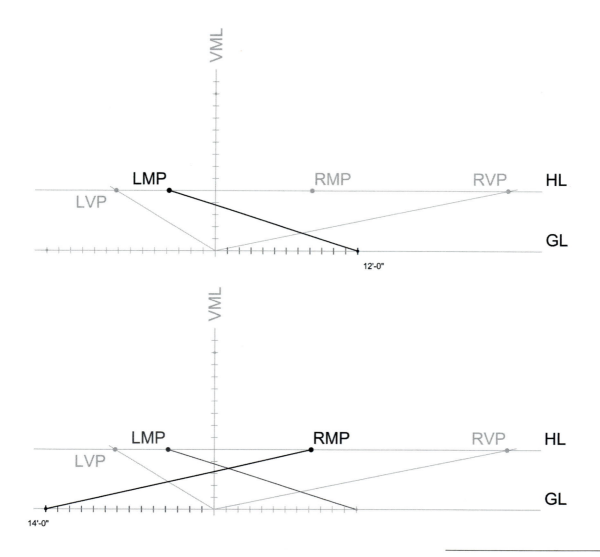

- The intersections of the measuring-point lines with the vanishing-point lines demarcate the new measurements that you will use to create the floor plane of the perspective.

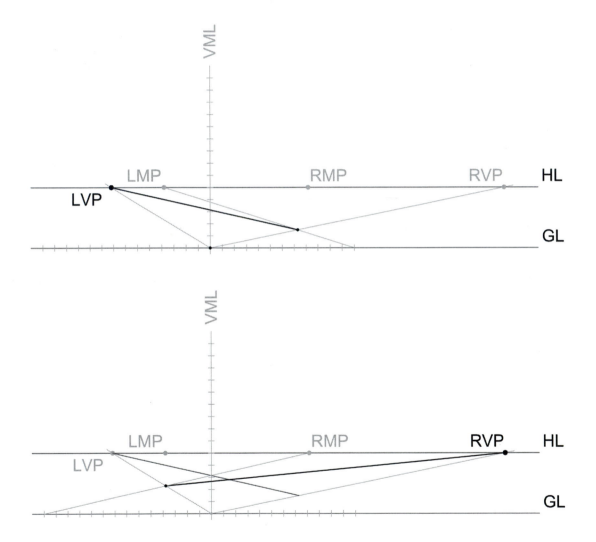

- This is the final floor plane.

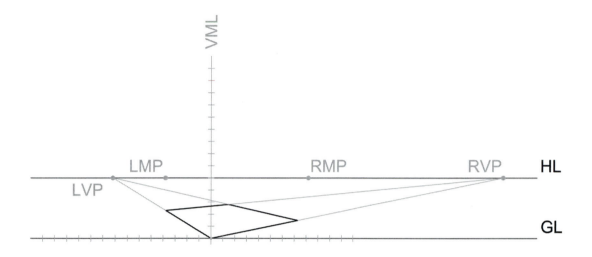

TIP: You might want to use a new piece of tracing paper to draw just what is needed to move forward with the perspective drawing. Your new drawing should keep the floor plane and the following:

- Ground line (GL)
- Horizon line (HL)
- Vertical measuring line (VML)
- Left and right vanishing points (LVP and RVP)
- Left and right measuring points (LMP and RMP)
- Floor plane

16. Using your T-square and the 90-degree side of your triangle, draw a vertical line at each of the intersections of the other three corners of the room.

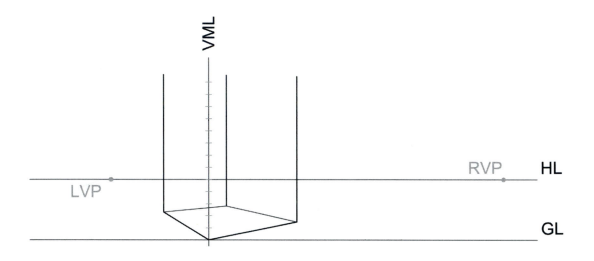

17. Measure the overall height of the space on the vertical measuring line.

- Draw a line from each vanishing point to the 13'-0" tick mark on the vertical measuring line to get the overall height of the front of the room.

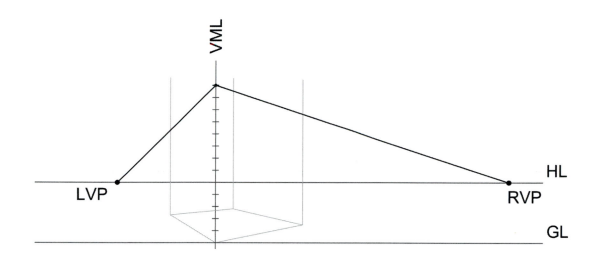

- Draw a line from each vanishing point to the new intersection of the line extending from the opposite vanishing point with the height of the back wall.
- Trim the lines to create the overall rectilinear space. The shaded planes are the floor and ceiling.

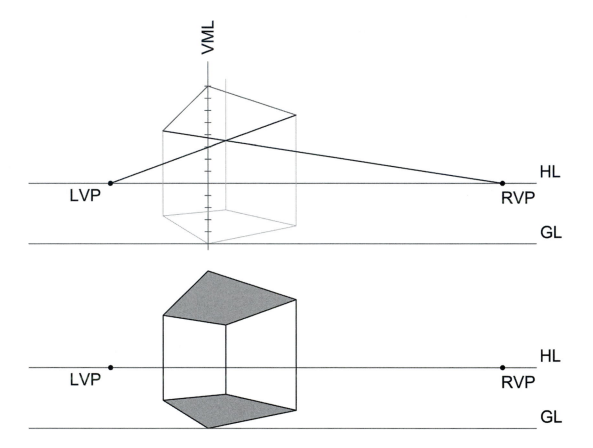

18. Translate the sloped ceiling information from the orthographic drawings to the perspective drawing.

- The walls on the north and south sides are 10'-0" high. Use the vertical measuring line to add these wall heights.

- Draw a line from each vanishing point to the 10'-0" mark on the vertical measuring line. At each new intersection of these lines with a back wall, draw lines from the opposite vanishing point.

- The shaded plane indicates the 10'-0"-high ceiling line.

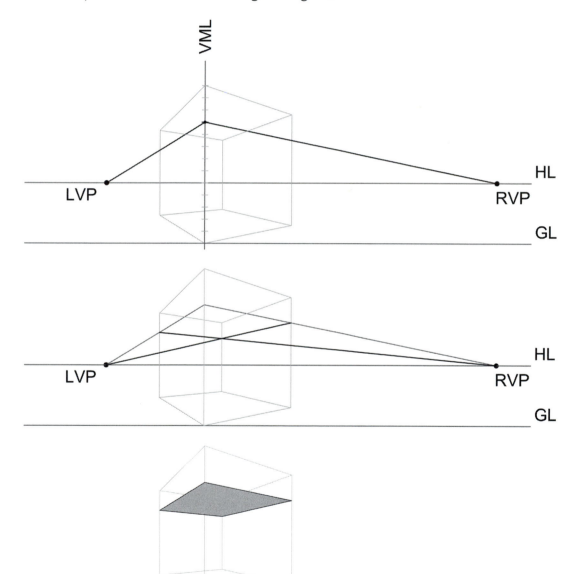

- The 13'-0"-high peak of the ceiling is located 3'-0" from the south wall, as is indicated by the dashed line on the floor plan. Draw a line from the 3'-0" measurement on the ground line to the left measuring point.

- Draw a line from the left vanishing point through the intersection on the floor plane.

- Using your T-square and triangle, "locked and loaded," draw a vertical line to the ceiling from the intersection of this new line on the back wall.

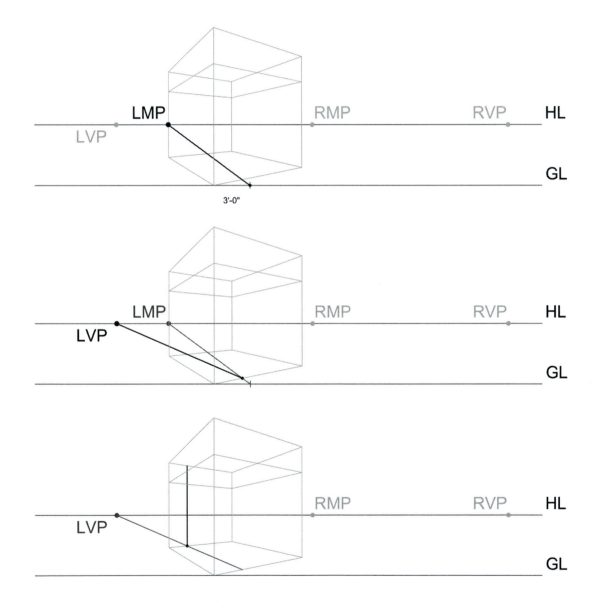

- With a straightedge, connect the heights on the back wall to create the angled ceilings. They will not be standard angles.
- Draw a line from the left vanishing point, through the peak of the ceiling, to the "invisible" front wall.

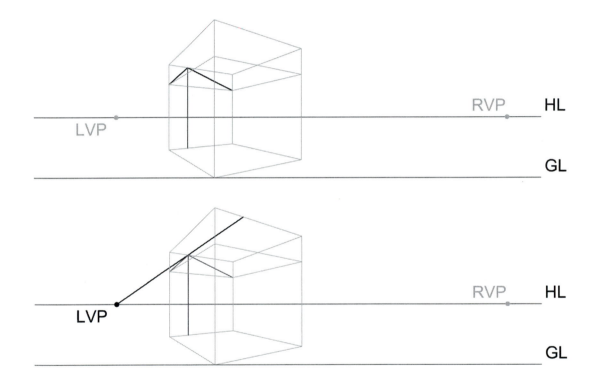

- Draw lines from the peak of the ceiling to the corners of the 10'-0"-high ceiling plane to connect the heights on the front wall.

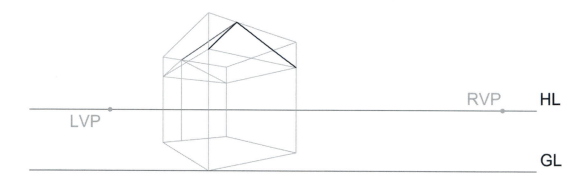

- Since we only want to see the space within the cone of vision for the perspective drawing, we can eliminate the planes that make up the left-side wall and ceiling to reveal the space within.

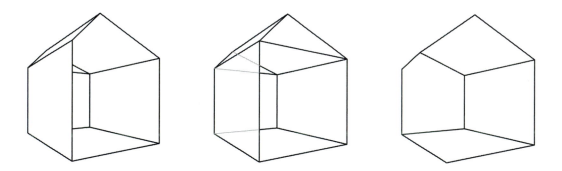

TIP: It might be best to start with a new piece of tracing paper after each major step is complete. Trace only what you need to use to continue your perspective, but do not throw away the other pages. It can be helpful to go back through them if you discover a problem later to see where things went wrong. This will also help you learn to draw more accurately.

You now have the basic shell of a two-point-perspective, which you can use to locate other items in the space. Similar to the one-point-perspective, these items can include architectural elements all the way through entourage. The following steps will vary depending on the space you want to draw, but the process will be very similar.

TWO-POINT-PERSPECTIVE DRAWING

To use the two-point-perspective drawing:

1. Start with a clean piece of tracing paper with the basic two-point perspective and each of the following:

   - Ground line (GL)

   - Horizon line (HL)

   - Vertical measuring line (VML)
     (*Remember to use this line for any height you need throughout the perspective.*)

   - Left and right vanishing points (LVP and RVP)

   - Left and right measuring points (LMP and RMP)

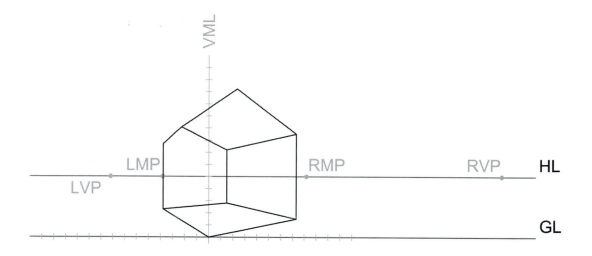

2. Subdivide the space, beginning with the major architectural and interior elements. Measure them on the orthographic drawings and translate them onto the perspective drawing, using lightly drawn lines.

- The orthographic drawings indicate that the fireplace and built-in shelving have a depth of 1'-9" off the west wall.

- Use the ground line to translate the 1'-9" onto the floor plane, following the same steps described previously to locate the ceiling peak, beginning with the right measuring point and followed by the right vanishing point.

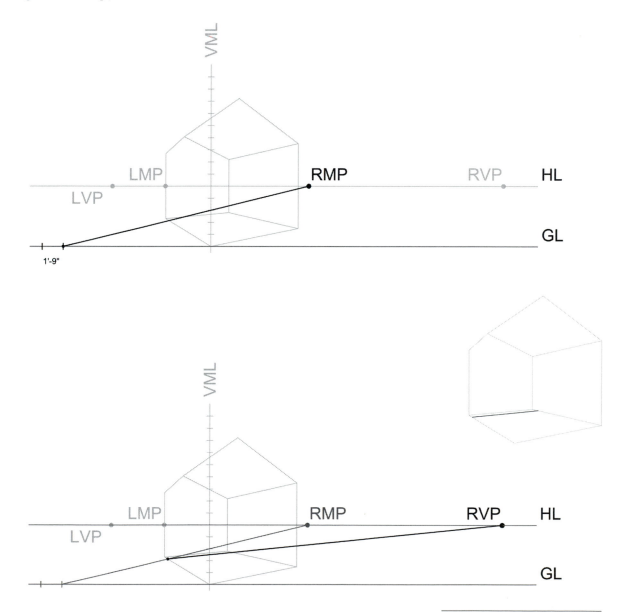

- The plan indicates that the fireplace is located 3'-0" off both the north and south walls, with a 4'-0"-wide firebox centered in the fireplace. The firebox has a 1½" trim within the 4'-0" opening.

- Using the ground line, translate these measurements onto the floor plane. In this case, you will use the left measuring and vanishing points.

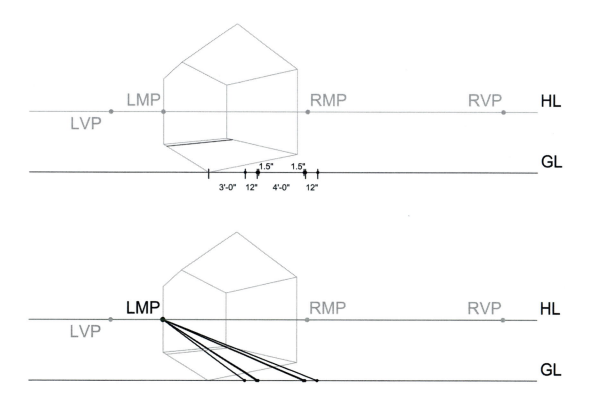

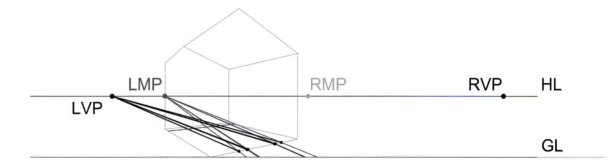

- Trim the lines to reveal the fireplace, the firebox with trim, and the built-in shelving on the floor plane.

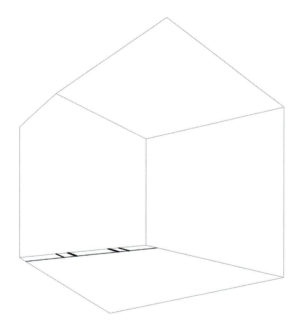

- Add the height to create the overall skeleton of the fireplace. We know from the orthographic drawings that the fireplace is 10'-0" tall. We also know that the firebox is located 1'-4" above the floor and is 1'-6" tall. The firebox has the same 1½" trim on the top and bottom.

- Use the vertical measuring line and left vanishing point to translate these measurements, just as in the previous steps. You do not need to locate the 10'-0" dimension since it is already established by the walls.

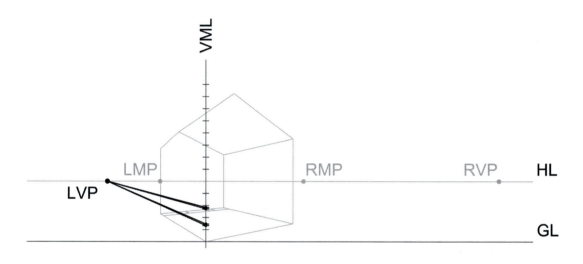

- Where these measurements intersect the edge of the picture plane, draw lines to the right vanishing point to translate the fireplace heights across the back wall.
  - Trim the lines to appear only across the length of the back wall.
  - Draw lines up from each intersection at the wall line on the floor plane using your 90-degree triangle.
  - Trim the lines to reflect just the elevation of the fireplace on the back wall.

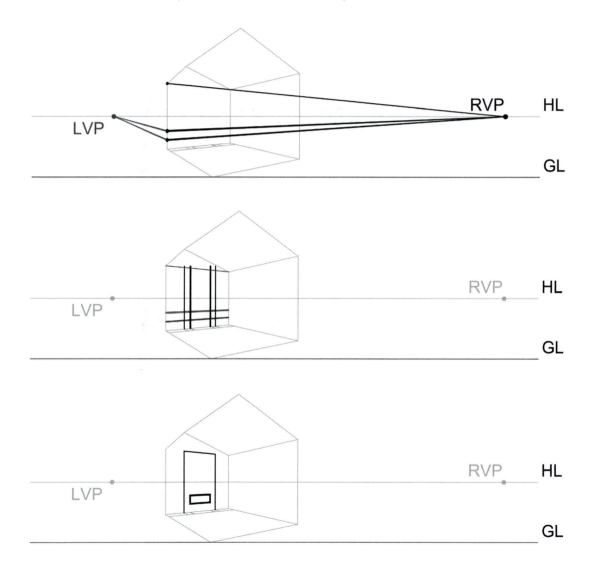

- To create the full volume of the fireplace, draw vertical lines from the two front points of the fireplace using your 90-degree triangle. Then, draw lines from the left vanishing point through each of the top corners of the fireplace on the back wall, intersecting with the vertical lines just drawn.

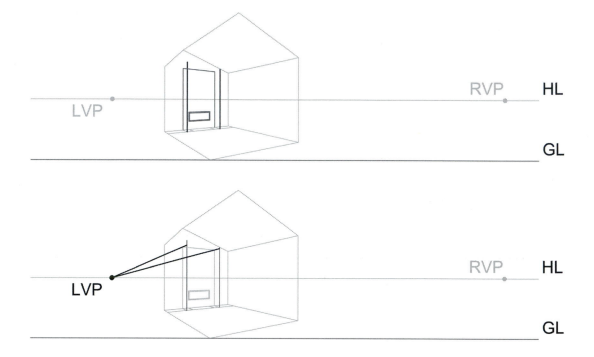

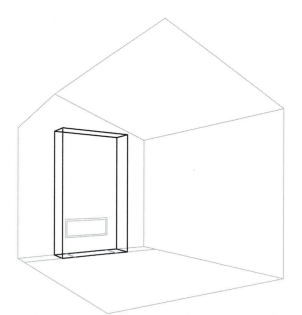

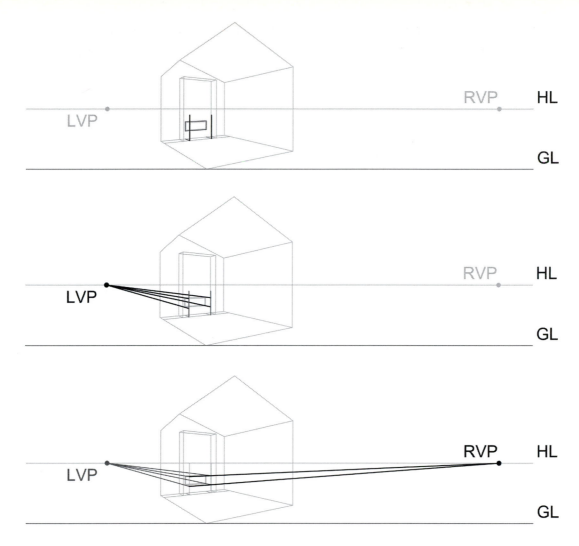

- Trace the outline of the fireplace and repeat the previous steps to create the firebox and depth on the fireplace.

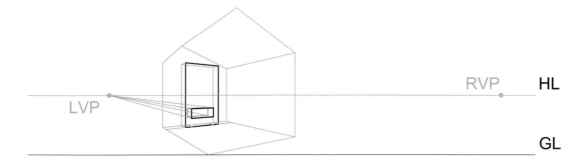

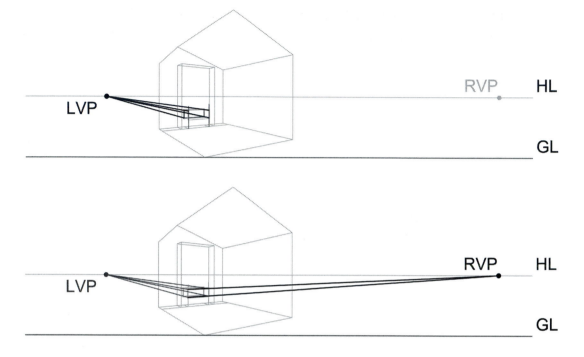

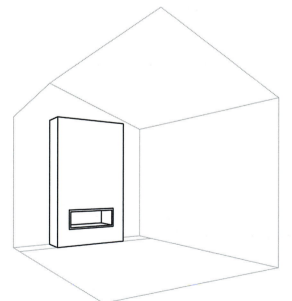

3. Repeat step 2 to add additional architectural elements.

- Add the windows on the north wall. The orthographic drawings indicate that the windows begin 3'-6" off the west wall. There are three 2'-4" windows, each with 2" frames, followed by a 2'-6" door, also with a 2" frame.

- Use the ground line to translate these dimensions onto the floor plane by following the previous steps, beginning with the right measuring point and followed by the right vanishing point.

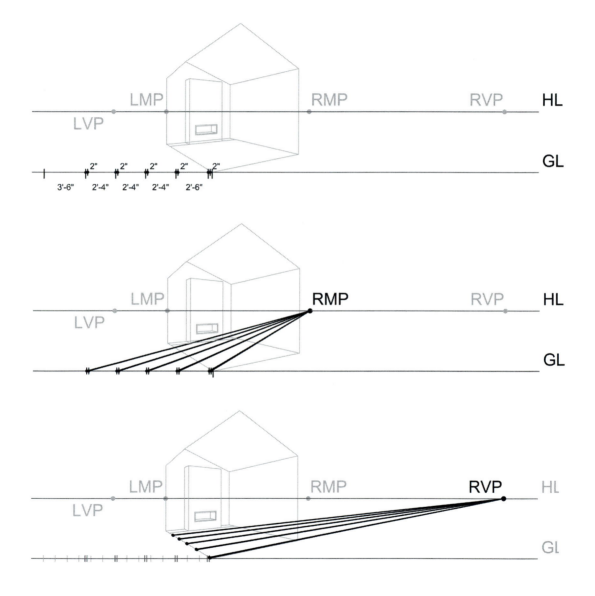

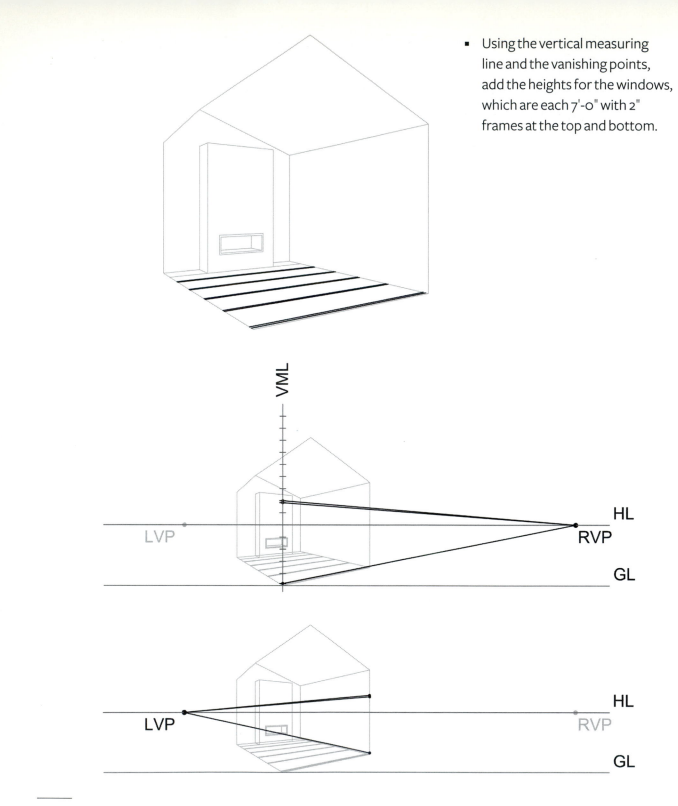

- Using the vertical measuring line and the vanishing points, add the heights for the windows, which are each 7'-0" with 2" frames at the top and bottom.

- Draw lines up from each intersection at the north wall line on the floor plane using your 90-degree triangle.
- Trim the lines to reflect just the elevation of the windows on the north wall.
  - Note that there is no bottom trim at the door location.

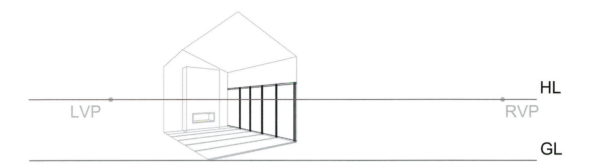

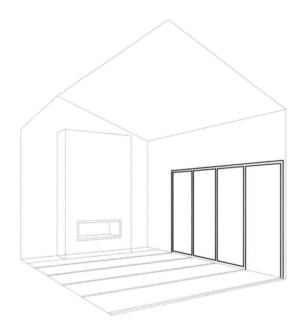

4. Add other built-in elements to the drawing. With this level of detail you should start with a new piece of tracing paper for each major element, then combine them in the end.

- Add the built-in shelving on both sides of the fireplace.

    - First, use the line from the front of the fireplace to locate the depth of the shelving (1'-9"). Using your 90-degree triangle, draw vertical lines from these points on the floor plane.

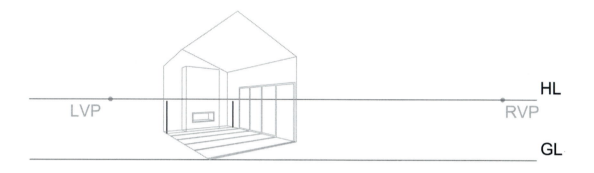

    - Second, locate the measurements of the individual shelves on the vertical measuring line. The bottoms of the shelves are located 1'-2", 2'-6", and 3'-10" above the floor and are 2" thick.

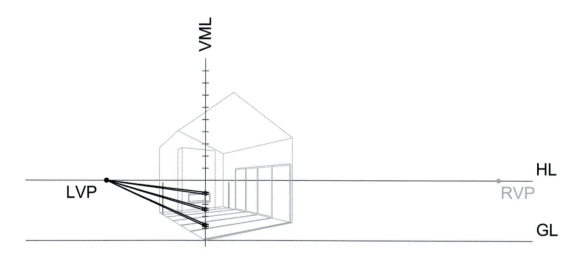

- Lastly, connect the shelves to the back wall using the left and right vanishing points.

- Close-ups are shown here to demonstrate the completion of the shelving to the south of the fireplace. The same method should be followed to complete the shelving on the north side.

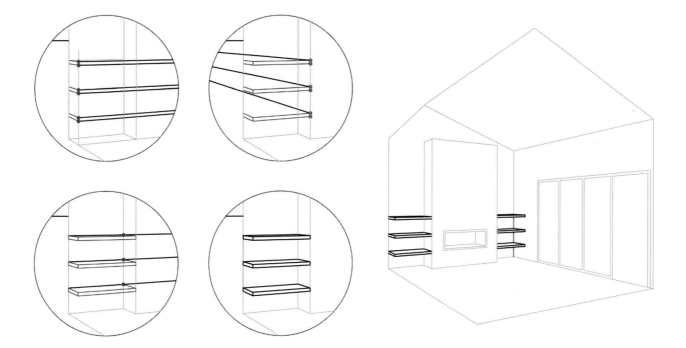

- Add the depth of the north wall. For this portion of the drawing, start with another piece of tracing paper and trace the window frames all the way down to the floor line. You will see how this will help us as the steps progress.

- The wall is 9" deep. Since the room is 12'-0" wide, locate a dimension of 12'-9" on the ground line and follow the previous steps.

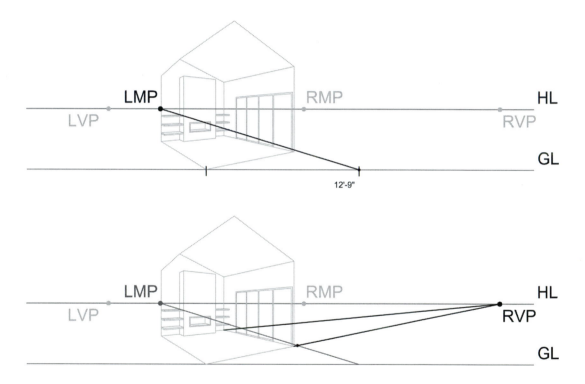

- You will have to extend the "front wall" line to the right vanishing point in order to translate the dimension of the wall's depth. To save time, also extend the structure's farthest point into the depth of the space to the right vanishing point. This will provide an understanding of the depth all the way down the north wall.

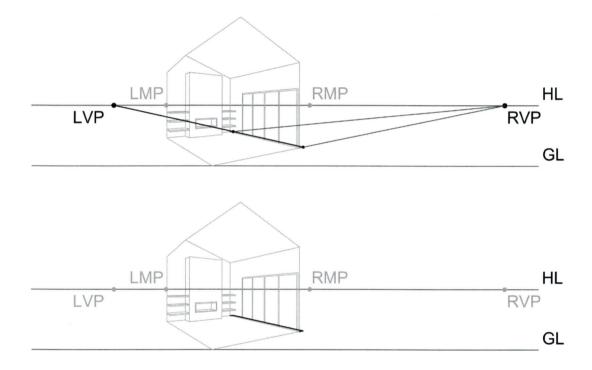

- Next, add the depth to the window frames. Perform these steps for the farthest window in the depth of the space. Once you have established the depth there, it is set for the entire wall. This is a very detailed effort, so the drawings have been enlarged for better understanding.

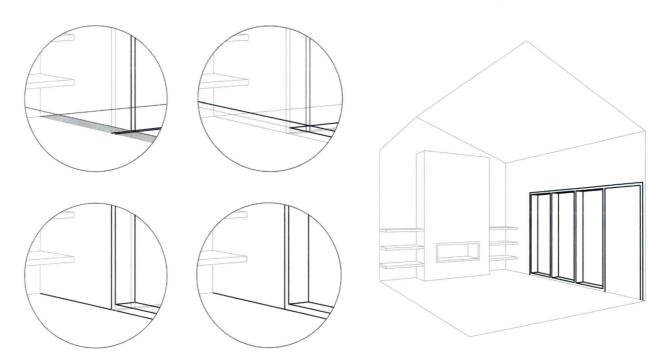

5. Add depth and detail to the drawing, including finishes and trim work.

- The baseboard on the walls is 3" high, and the wood cladding on the fireplace is spaced 3" apart. Both can be measured on the vertical measuring line and then translated onto the walls and fireplace.

- Translate the heights from the vertical measuring line to a vertical line at the 1'-9" depth, which is the front of the fireplace wall.

- Next, draw lines across the fireplace to the right vanishing point.

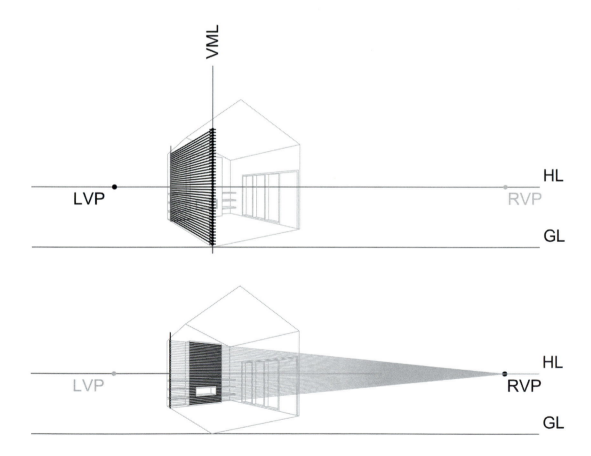

- Finally, "wrap" the wood cladding around the fireplace using the left vanishing point and create the base board in a similar way.

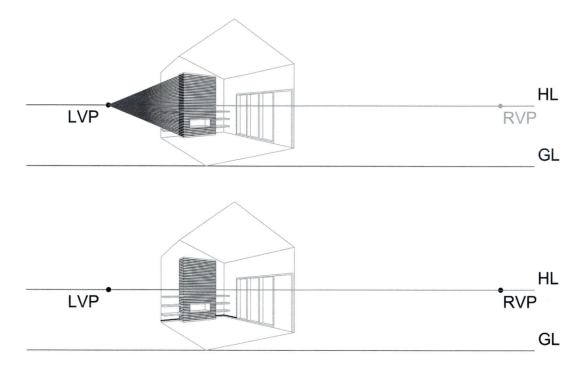

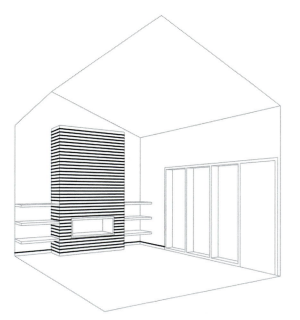

TIP: You can simplify the process by only drawing on the face of the fireplace when lining up your straightedge to the right vanishing point. To make things even easier, you can also eliminate the lines that would have been drawn over the firebox.

6. Finally, add furniture and people, or entourage, into the space to make it feel more realistic, remembering to put a person's "eyes" on the horizon line.

    ▪ As with all the architectural and interior elements in the previous steps, draw the furniture on the floor plane first, then add the height, and, finally, the detail.

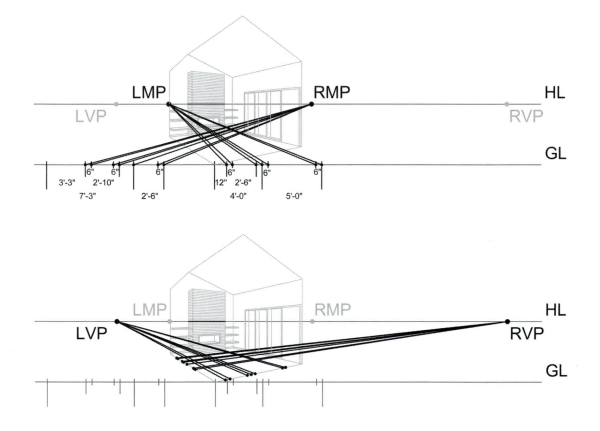

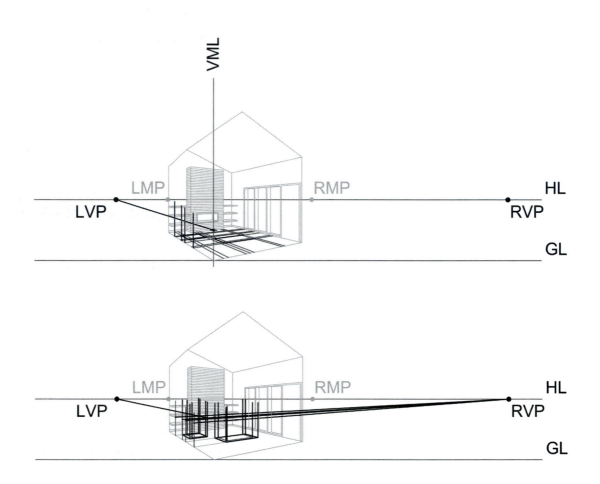

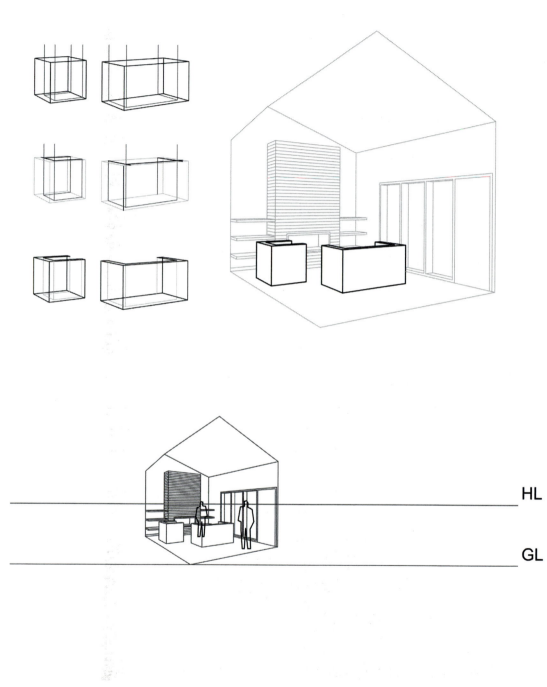

To truly finish the perspective, you should trace it one last time and add line weights. Refer to Chapter Two in Book Two of the Studio Companion Series, *Drafting Basics,* to review line weights. In addition to line weights, you can crop the drawing where the 60-degree cone of vision dictates to make it feel as if you are in the space.

You can increase or decrease the size of the final drawing with a copier, allowing you to customize the size to fit your presentation.

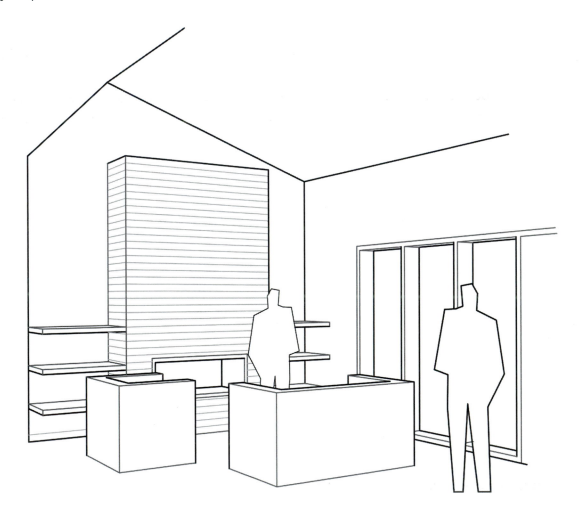

EXERCISE

||||||||||||||||||||||||||||||||||||||||||||||||||||||||||||||||||||||||||||||||||||||||||||||||||||||||||||||||||||

TOOLS NEEDED

Drafting board

Drafting brush

Drafting dots

Dry cleaning pad

Lead holder

Lead pointer

Leads

Scale

Tracing paper

Triangles

T-square

Set up your drafting area and prepare to draw a two-point perspective of the kitchen of the one-bedroom cabin.

1. Tape a copy of your floor plan onto your drafting board at a 30/60-degree angle, with drafting dots at all four corners. Then, tape a large piece of tracing paper over the top and perform the following steps.

2. Determine what you want to see in your two-point perspective and locate the following:

   - Picture plane (PP)

   - Station point or standing point (SP)

   - Central axis of vision (CAV)

   - Left and right vanishing points (LVP and RVP)

   - Left and right measuring points (LMP and RMP)

   - Cone of vision (COV)

3. Draw the picture plane as explained in this chapter and note the following:

   - Picture plane (PP)

   - Ground line (GL)

   - Horizon line (HL)

   - Vertical measuring line (VML)

   - Left and right vanishing points (LVP and RVP)

   - Left and right measuring points (LMP and RMP)

4. Using lightly drawn lines, create the perspective for the overall room.
5. Follow the step-by-step directions to complete the drawing of the kitchen in the one-bedroom cabin.

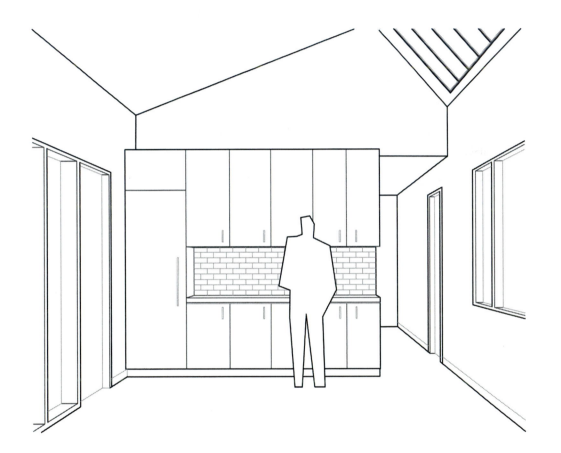

TIPS

- Accuracy is the most important thing in drawing the perspective. Making sure your measurements are correct will benefit you in the long run.

  - Make sure you work from the measuring points first, then the vanishing points, when creating the drawing.

  - Create the overall shape of the space first, then add the major elements, and, finally, the details.

- Use multiple pieces of tracing paper to help clarify the drawing as you work, and keep those papers so that you can review them if you find a mistake later on.

- Use different colored highlighters on a copy of the perspective to determine line weights before you do the final drawing.

EVALUATION

- Does the final drawing appear to be square and true? If not, review your tracing-paper layers to see if you can identify where you made a mistake, while reviewing the steps of the process again.

- Does each element within the perspective appear to be parallel and equal in proportion to the orthographic drawings? If not, again review your tracing papers to see if you can determine where the drawing went wrong.

- Ask a fellow student to review your work, or look at your drawing upside down to see if you can spot a mistake.

SUMMARY

Two-point perspectives are a great way to gain an inside understanding of a space because they use human scale in their creation, and they are more realistic with two vanishing points. Drawing two-point perspectives is a difficult skill to learn, but you will master it with continued practice.

FOUR

MODEL-BUILDING TOOLS AND SUPPLIES

OBJECTIVES

You will be able to identify and successfully use:

- The basic tools for model building
- The basic supplies for model building

NO DOUBT YOU HAVE PURCHASED A SET OF TOOLS, USUALLY REFERRED TO AS A *KIT,* OF THE BASIC EQUIPMENT YOU WILL NEED IN YOUR FIRST YEAR OF STUDY OF ARCHITECTURE AND INTERIOR DESIGN. MOST OF THESE TOOLS ARE USED FOR TECHNICAL DRAFTING, BUT SOME ARE ALSO USED FOR BUILDING MODELS. IN THIS CHAPTER WE WILL DISCUSS THE TOOLS AND SUPPLIES USED FOR MODEL BUILDING; BOOK TWO OF THE STUDIO COMPANION SERIES, *DRAFTING BASICS,* ADDRESSES THE TOOLS USED FOR DRAFTING.

THE TOOLS USED TO BUILD MODELS ARE TRIED AND TRUE AND WILL ALLOW YOU TO CREATE BEAUTIFUL WORK. LEARNING THE CORRECT NAME AND USE FOR EACH TOOL IS CRITICAL, NOT ONLY FOR SUCCESS IN MODEL BUILDING BUT FOR YOUR SAFETY AS WELL.

CUTTING TOOLS

There are several types of cutting tools for model building, with many different names, but this section will look at the two major categories: knives and cutters. Each offers heavy- and light-duty styles, as well as retractable models that vary by blade type.

Consider the material, thickness, and final, finished edge of the product you are cutting when selecting the proper tool to use.

With only one exception, which will be mentioned later, always cut with the blade perpendicular to the material you are cutting, and pull the blade toward you to achieve crisp, clean edges.

If your cuts are not crisp, it is time to change the blade. Do not try to muscle the cut—this will result in a ragged edge, and you run the risk of hurting yourself. Also, if you hear a click, the point of the blade has been damaged, so replace the blade.

As with many skills, practicing with these tools will increase your accuracy and success with the finished product. Remember to always practice safety when using cutting tools. This includes disposal of used blades, as well as their safe storage when not in use.

CRAFT AND X-ACTO KNIVES

The most common knife for model building is an art-and-hobby knife that uses a #11 blade. These knives are produced by several different manufacturers, but they are most commonly referred to as *x-acto knives,* similar to how we often call a copy a Xerox or a facial tissue a Kleenex. Regardless of what you call it, this all-purpose knife can cut paper, balsa and basswood, acetate, matboard, museum board, and foam-core board. These art-and-hobby knives are available with a standard knife handle or in a fingertip version.

The #5 heavy-duty x-acto knife is compatible with ten different blades, each associated with a specific material and task. This tool may be used depending on the type of model you are building.

X-acto knives come with several features, but the following three are crucial: an antislip or ergonomic grip, a non-roll collar, and a safety cap. These features help to ensure your comfort and safety when using and storing the knife.

To change the blade, simply twist the end of the knife while carefully holding the blade in place. Then, remove and properly dispose of the blade, and replace it by inserting a new blade into the slot, reversing the procedure.

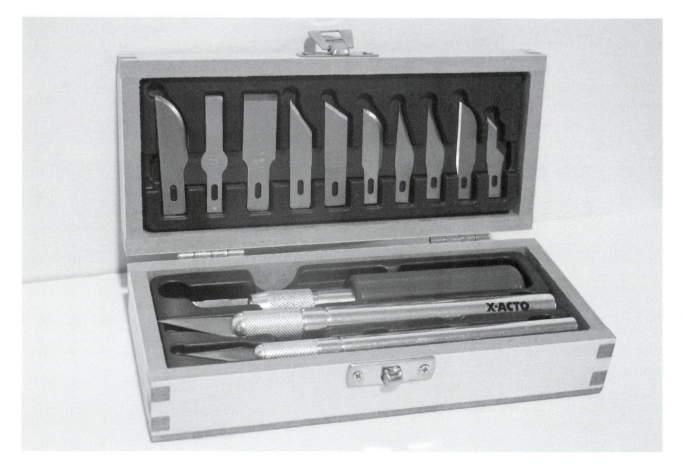

UTILITY KNIVES

Utility knives are very similar to x-acto knives, but they are used for more heavy-duty materials and typically have retractable blades and metal handles. They do a good job cutting through materials but do not offer as much control as an x-acto knife.

To change the blade on a utility knife, open up the knife to expose the cutting blade and to find the replacement blades, which are commonly stored inside the handle. The first time that you need to change the blade, you can simply flip over the first blade and use the opposite end. The second time, you will replace the blade with a new one.

Some utility knives have snap-off blades. These are also good for basic cutting, but replacing the blade is more difficult. When snapping off an old blade, it is possible to damage the edge of the new one, so do so carefully.

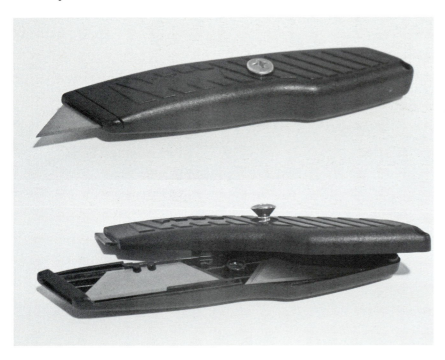

OTHER KNIVES

Two other knives for model building are worth mentioning. First is the swivel knife, which features a blade that can rotate 360 degrees and is used to cut fairly tight curves. These are available with a standard knife handle and in a fingertip version. The second is a wood-carving knife. As its name implies, this knife is for cutting wood. Due to its concave blade, it provides greater precision than a craft knife.

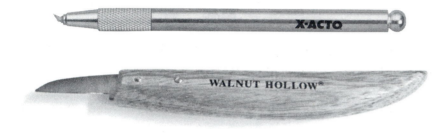

ROTARY CUTTERS

Rotary cutters feature a circular blade and can be used for light-duty cutting of paper and specialty papers for model building. They should not be used for cutting any board because they will crush the surface.

CIRCLE CUTTERS

There are two options for cutting circles. The first is a compass cutter. This tool is used just like a traditional drafting compass, but there is a blade on the end of the stylus where there would normally be lead. Compass cutters are adjustable up to 12" on some models and have built-in rulers for accuracy. Use great care when cutting with this tool and focus on keeping the blade perpendicular to what you are cutting.

The second option is a circle cutter, which operates in a similar manner to the compass cutter. There are specific circle cutters for paper and foam-core board. Make sure you select the correct one for the material you are cutting.

FOAM-CORE BOARD CUTTING TOOLS

There are special tools to assist with cutting foam-core board that create clean and crisp cuts.

RABBET CUTTER

This cutter creates a rabbeted edge on one side of a 90-degree corner of foam-core board. It removes one side of the paper and the foam-core center, leaving just the rigid paper on the second side. This allows us to create a corner joint that has no foam exposed along the edge. To form the rabbet joint, place the edge of a clean piece of foam-core board against the rigid paper edge that was left behind by the rabbet cutter. Simply add a bead of glue and hold the pieces together for a few seconds to produce a clean square corner.

BEVEL OR 45-DEGREE CUTTER

Another method for creating a 90-degree corner on a model is to use a 45-degree miter joint. A bevel cutter allows you to cut an edge at a 45-degree angle with the use of an attachment that keeps the bottom of the tool at an angle as it runs along the surface of the foam-core board while the blade cuts the board edge.

To form the miter-joint corner, two pieces of board must have the 45-degree beveled edge. The boards are then assembled in the same manner as the rabbet-joint corner.

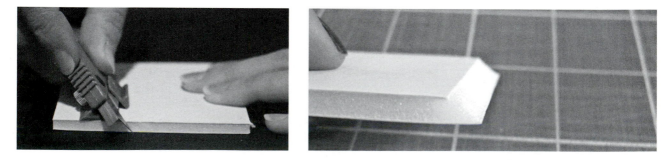

FOAMWERKS

There is a line of tools for cutting foam-core board, called FoamWerks, by Logan Graphic Products. Each tool features an ergonomic handle with accommodations for right- and left-handed users. They have internal blade storage in each tool and easily adjustable blades for different board thicknesses.

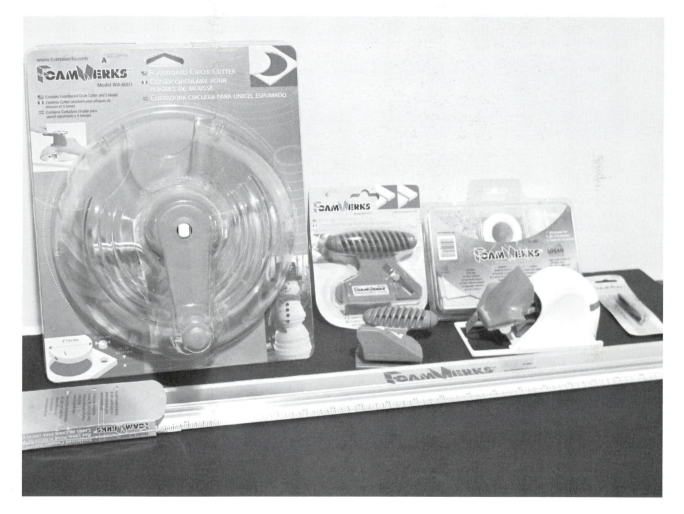

The FoamWerks line includes:

- Straight cutter—
  This tool cuts just like an x-acto knife, but it offers more control for cutting through thicker foam-core boards.

- Straight/bevel cutter—
  This is an all-in-one tool for straight and bevel cuts.

- Rabbet cutter—
  Cuts rabbet joints only.

- Circle cutter—
  Cuts circles up to 6" in diameter and ½" deep.

- V-groove cutter—
  This tool cuts a "V" into the surface of the foam-core board, allowing you to bend and curve the foam core without disturbing the rigid paper surface on the opposite side. It features an adjustable blade to accommodate board up to ½" thick.

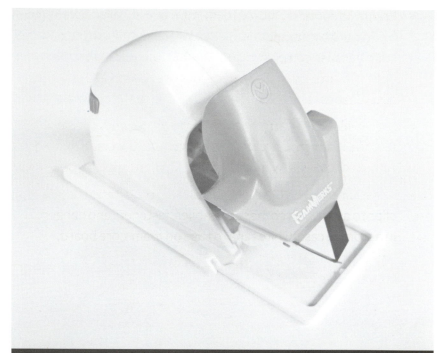

- Freestyle cutter—This tool cuts any free-form shape into the foam-core board, and it is much more successful than an x-acto knife because you push the tool away from yourself, rather than pull it toward yourself, resulting in more control and cleaner cuts. Shapes can be cut out of the middle of the board as well.

- Hole drill—This tool allows you to cut ¼", ½", and ¾" holes into the foam-core board. It also dispenses the circle that was removed to create the hole, which can then be used elsewhere.

- Accessories and replacement blades—These items include clips to assist with corner assemblies, fasteners and hangers in a storage case, white tape for use on foam-core board, replacement blades for each cutter, and a channel rail to use as a straightedge with all the cutting tools.

OTHER CUTTING TOOLS

There are other tools made specifically to assist with wood, metal, and plastics that create clean and crisp cuts.

MIGHTY CUTTER

This scissorlike tool cuts balsa and basswood strips up to ½" thick at angles ranging from 45 degrees to 120 degrees. Simply turn the mechanism to the desired angle and squeeze the handle.

THE CHOPPER

This tool produces straight 30-, 45-, and 60-degree-angle cuts of wood and plastic strips using a lever arm with a razor blade. It also has movable stops to assist in creating duplicate model pieces quickly and accurately.

RAZOR SAW AND MITER BOX

The small miter box is metal with slots to provide 45-degree and 90-degree cuts up to $7/8$" thick, using a razor saw, for metal, wood, and plastic. The miter box has a small lip that allows it to rest snugly against a tabletop edge. The floor of the box has grooves to hold several different sizes of materials in place while they are cut.

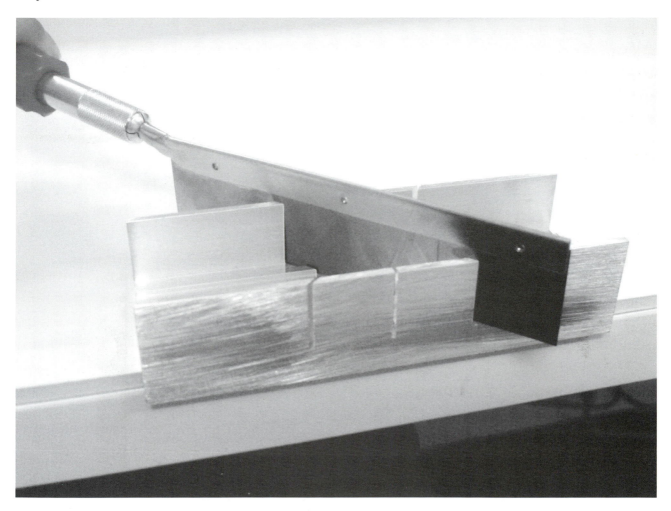

SELF-HEALING MATS

A protective mat should be used when cutting, to protect the work surface below. Self-healing mats provide a nonglare, grid-and-angle-lined surface to cut upon, and the translucent versions can be used on light tables. The mats come in a range of colors and sizes, and you may want a variety as you build your model-building tools kit.

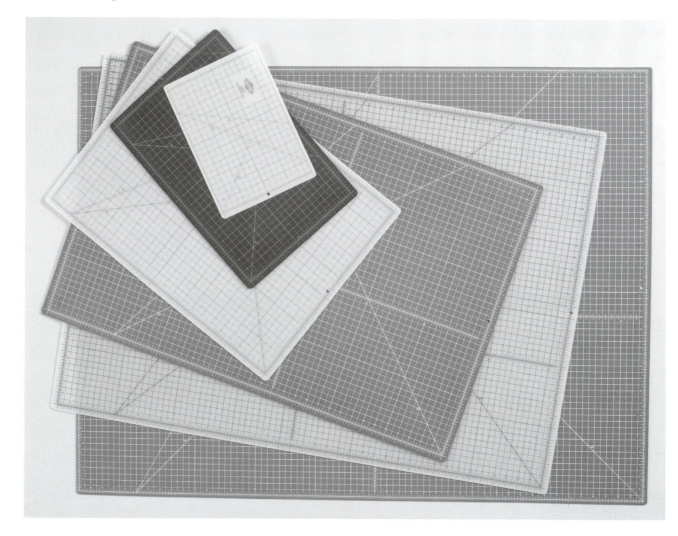

METAL CORK-BACKED TRIANGLES AND RULERS

These tools allow you to cut along them without damaging the surface of the tool. The cork-backed feature keeps the tool from slipping while cutting, and the triangles can be used with a T-square to ensure the proper angle is achieved. Nonetheless, a cutting mat should always be used underneath to protect the work surface. Never cut against a T-square because it could damage the edge and then, when it's used to draft, the lines could have dips or unevenness as a result.

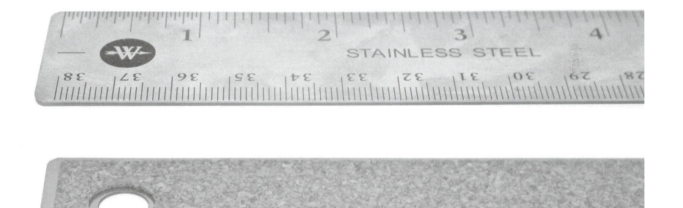

BUILDING MATERIALS

For rip-and-tear models or study models, which will be discussed in the next chapter, literally anything can be used, and recycled or reused materials are just fine. As long as you can cut and shape it, you can use it.

PAPER

Any kind of paper can be used to create models, from regular copy and bond paper to textured and colored paper.

For white models, heavier paper can be used. The rule is that the paper must hold its shape and stand on its own without assistance.

Different colored papers can be used to create final models, but they are typically reserved to represent different materials within the model. A gray paper can be used to represent concrete, or a highly textured paper can be used to represent rocks or carpeting.

BOARDS

There are five types of board that can be used for model building, and they include: foam-core board, museum board, chipboard, matboard, and cardboard. The first three boards are used the most. Matboard and cardboard can be used for study models, but they typically would not be the material of choice for models seen by the client, unless it is in the very early stages of the design process.

FOAM-CORE BOARD

Foam-core is a lightweight board made of a polystyrene foam center laminated with coated paper on both sides. Typically it comes in solid white or black, but color-faced board is available. A standard sheet is $\frac{3}{16}$" thick, but ranges from $\frac{1}{8}$" to $\frac{1}{2}$" thick. Foam-core board is easy to cut and assemble.

MUSEUM BOARD

Museum board comes in sheets at three different thicknesses: 2 ply, 4 ply, and 8 ply. The thickness is selected based on the scale of the model you are creating. The color is consistent throughout the thickness of the board, and, due to its manufacturing process, it is free of specks, dirt, and blemishes, making it excellent for model building. Museum board is 100 percent cotton, is easy to cut, and accepts glue beautifully.

CHIPBOARD

Chipboard is an inexpensive alternative to museum board, at about a quarter of the cost. It has a brown or gray color throughout the thickness of the board and comes in 14 ply and 30 ply. The color is not consistent from one manufacturing to the next because it is made from recycled materials, so always purchase enough to complete the entire project as new sheets could be a different color and become distracting in the model.

OTHER BUILDING MATERIALS

BALSA WOOD AND BASSWOOD

Balsa wood is light and soft, making it easy to cut and shape with an x-acto knife. It is available in sheets, rods, and strips, and it finishes nicely with paint or can be left bare.

Basswood is harder than balsa wood but is still easily used for model building. It also comes in sheets, rods, and strips and finishes well. Due to the dense nature of basswood, a razor saw might be needed to cut thicker pieces.

ACETATE AND DURA-LAR

Acetate and Dura-Lar are clear materials used to represent glass and other transparent items in models. They come in different thicknesses and are fairly easy to cut. You may want a special plastic cutter for Dura-Lar, but you can use an x-acto knife—it will just take several passes to cut through the material.

PLASTIC

Molded and extruded plastic strips, rods, and structural shapes can have a variety of uses in models. They are fairly easy to cut, depending on the shape, and they are very rigid.

METAL

Aluminum and brass are metals that can be used for model building. They come in sheets, tubes, rods, bars, mesh, and wire. Most can be cut with wire cutters or shears; however, there is a special tool to cut and bend metal tubes due to their delicate nature.

SUPPLIES

TACKY GLUE

Tacky glue is the best glue to use for model building. It is an all-purpose glue that is easy to control, sets up quickly, and dries clear. There are other glues that you can try, each with different advantages, but tacky glue seems to possess all of them in one product.

GLUE STICKS AND ADHESIVE RUNNERS

Glue sticks and adhesive runners are a good choice for rip-and-tear models, but not for any other. They just don't have the longevity that tacky glue has.

HOT-GLUE GUNS

Hot-glue guns should not be used for model building. They are hard to control, leave glue strings, and add unwanted bulk to models. In addition, they tend to fail rather quickly and leave stains behind.

DRAFTING DOTS AND TAPE

Drafting tape can be used to temporarily assist with gluing a study model, or for rip-and-tear models. It is also good for labeling pieces of the model while you cut them out. The tape peels off easily and does not damage the surface of the piece.

DOUBLE-SIDED TAPE

Double-sided tape comes in different widths and tackiness. It is great for rip-and-tear, study, and final models; just make sure to choose the correct tack for the materials used in the project.

BONE FOLDER

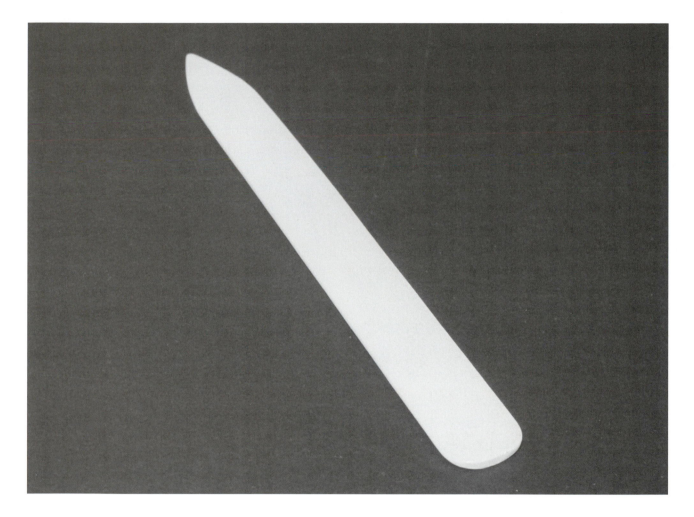

Bone folders are used to score and fold paper and museum board (up to 4 ply). To create a score, use the tip of the tool against a straightedge, applying gentle pressure as you go. To make a crisp fold, use the side of the bone folder to crease the paper at the score line, then smooth it across from end to end.

TOOL STORAGE

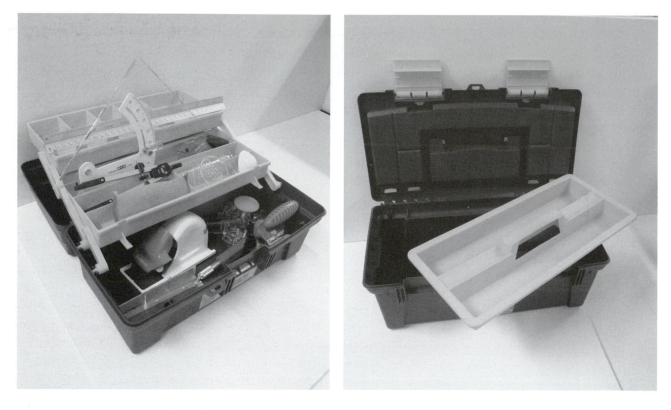

For safety reasons, some tools come with their own method of storage, such as a cap for an x-acto knife, for example. But you should store all of your tools together for easy access and convenience.

A common method of storage is to have a tackle box or art bin that has different compartments and levels to keep tools organized. Some people prefer to keep like tools together and use smaller organizers that are kept in a bag or drawer. Others prefer to use zippered bags to keep specific categories of tools together, such as all their drawing instruments or model-building tools. Regardless, the goal is to keep your tools clean and in working order.

Finally, you should put your initials on each tool, or mark them in some way to identify them as yours. Some people put nail polish on each tool or apply colored electrical tape, but no matter what the method, make sure it is for you exclusively so that you don't confuse your tools with someone else's.

SUMMARY

Learning the names and uses of your model-building tools allows you to create beautiful models and communicate your design ideas. Using the tools safely and for their intended use gives you the best chance for success in your model building.

FIVE

MODEL-BUILDING STRATEGIES

OBJECTIVES

You will be able to identify and successfully create the following types of models for use in the design process:

- Rip-and-tear models
- White models
- Finish models

MODELS ARE THREE-DIMENSIONAL, PHYSICAL REPRESENTATIONS CREATED TO ASSIST VIEWERS WITH AN UNDERSTANDING OF A SPACE, BUILDING, OR ITEM. THEY ARE CREATED, TYPICALLY TO A MEASURABLE SCALE, USING BUILDING TOOLS AND SUPPLIES, REFERENCING THE ORTHOGRAPHIC DRAWINGS. MODELS ARE AN EXCELLENT WAY TO EXPLORE AND PRESENT A DESIGN. THEY CAN BE A "DOWN AND DIRTY," RIP-AND-TEAR MODEL TO EXPLORE A SMALL IDEA OR A BEAUTIFULLY CRAFTED FINAL MODEL FOR A CLIENT PRESENTATION.

To fully understand all of the model-building strategies, as well as topics in Books Two, Three, and Four of the Studio Companion Series, the small one-bedroom cabin will be used throughout this chapter.

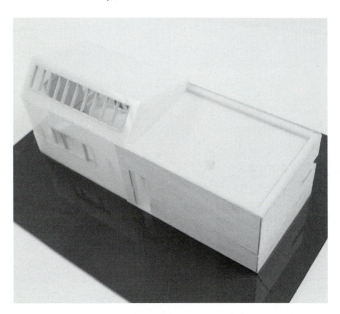

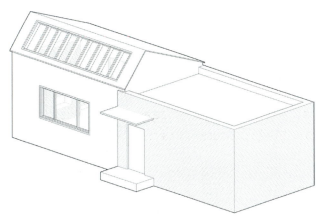

Additionally, images of Frank Gehry's design solution for the Guggenheim Museum Bilbao in Bilbao, Spain, will be included in this chapter, similar to other books in this series. The completed museum is shown here to reference as you examine the use of models during the design process in this chapter.

It is important to know all of the strategies to building a model; however, different academic programs focus on different methods in the first year of study. The names of these strategies also vary, but the overall goal is the same: to get the design idea from your head to your hands, so that all three dimensions can be explored and understood.

Finally, different academic programs allow for the extensive use of technology for model building, which can include equipment such as three-dimensional printers, laser cutters, CNC routers, etc., but I—and many others—believe that hand model-building skills should be taught as an essential part of a beginning design curriculum. This will remain a skill that you use throughout your education and well into your career. Taking the time to learn the basics now will benefit you greatly in the future.

RIP-AND-TEAR MODELS

||||||||||||||||||||||||||||||||||||||||||||||||||||||||||||||||||||||||||||||||||||||||||||||||||||||||||||||||||||||||||||||||||||

A basic design study can be explored by simply ripping and tearing paper. Common bond paper, found objects, or recycled products can be used in the process.

Rip-and-tear models may be referred to as *study models* or *massing models*. Their purpose is to quickly experiment with possibilities for your design. The more study models that you produce, the more ideas that will be generated, and the closer the design comes to a refined, well-thought-out concept.

Rip-and-tear models will routinely evolve, being ripped and torn from their original shapes, with items added or taken away as the process continues. Experimentation is the purpose of these models, and you should never get too attached to them.

Finally, rip-and-tear modeling can occur at several stages throughout the design process, but it typically takes place in the schematic-design and design-development phases. In the schematic-design phase, models most often demonstrate the "big idea," while models in the design-development phase usually focus on a specific area or portion of the project. Models from any of these phases may or may not be seen by the client.

A rip-and-tear model can indicate:

- The overall size and shape, or mass, of a building or object.

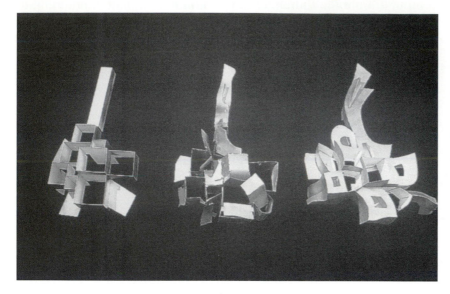

From left to right, this photo shows the initial rectilinear models indicating the overall massing of Frank Gehry's Guggenheim Museum Bilbao in Bilbao, Spain. These are just a few of the many study models used to create the final exterior design.

- The exploration of an idea for a portion of the overall design, including options for specific elements of the overall design, such as the change of materials from one form to another or studies for the roofline.

These two models explore the form, scale, and materiality for different portions of the design of the museum.

CREATING A RIP-AND-TEAR MODEL

To create a rip-and-tear model:

1. Using a scale, measure the height of the item you are designing on a piece of paper or board, then fold it to create the boundaries of the space.

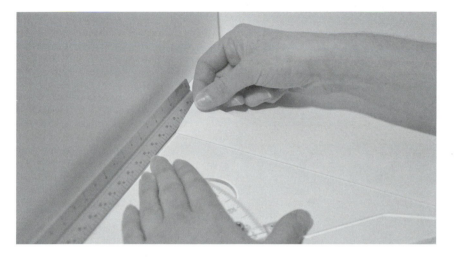

- Use tape, glue sticks, paper clips, or staples to make the model more rigid, or to make larger-size models.

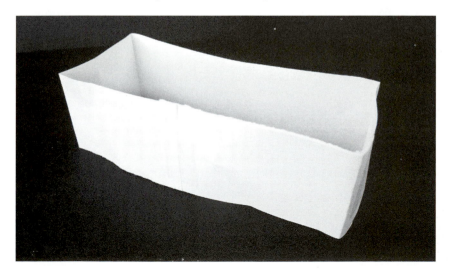

2. Create multiple models so that you can readily examine and compare different options.

- This can be something as simple as exploring wood-cladding options for the massing in the small one-bedroom cabin.

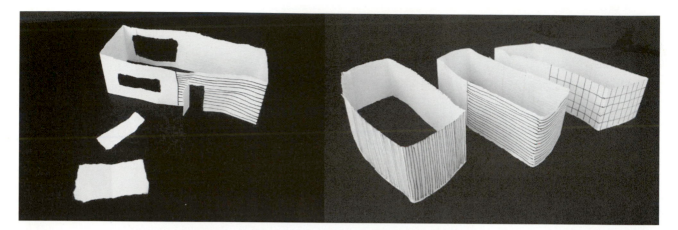

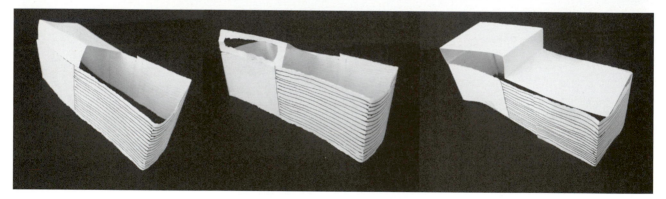

3. Carefully rip out any doors, windows, and openings so as to accurately represent your design idea.
4. Repeat these steps to create as many options as needed to exhaust all of the design opportunities for your project.

- The differences between models can be very subtle. Here is a study showing the impact of adding a skylight to the roofline, or using an angled roof versus a higher flat roof.

TIP: You can create an abundance of study models, but because they are fragile, you should photograph or sketch them to document your design process.

WHITE MODELS

White models are more formal than rip-and-tear models. They are created to scale with one material, typically white museum board. Additional materials, such as clear acetate for windows or balsa wood to indicate a material change, may be added for clarity.

There are two basic ways to create a white model. The first is to cut out each element of the design and then assemble the parts; the second is to fold or bend a portion of the design—for example, to create a staircase or a series of barrel vaults. One method might be preferred over the other for different portions of the final white model.

Finally, white models may be constructed at various stages throughout the design process, but they typically are made at the end of the schematic-design phase and throughout the design-development phase.

Just like a rip-and-tear model, a white model can indicate:

- The overall size and shape, or mass, of a building or object.

- The exploration of an idea for a portion of the overall design, including options for specific elements of the overall design.

- An understanding of human scale. Simple scaled figures (people) should be placed in or around the model to demonstrate the relationship of the project to a person.

The two model types differ because a white model is typically created after a design solution has been fleshed out. White models will more than likely be seen by the client, but may also just be utilized for the design team's understanding. The level of craft and technique is greater for a white model than for a rip-and-tear model.

CREATING A WHITE MODEL

To create a white model:

1. Typically, you will begin with the orthographic drawings. Using a scale, measure on your board the length, width, and height of each item within the design, and then cut out each piece.

   - These pieces would be the result of referring to the one-bedroom cabin.

2. Carefully cut out any doors, windows, and openings so as to accurately represent the orthographic drawings.

- Back each cut-out door and window with another piece of museum board so that you do not see into the unfinished center of the model.
- Lightly score window mullions or material changes like the wood cladding with an x-acto knife. These pieces of the model have examples of both. The skylight piece has scored mullions while the walls have solid ones with scored wood.

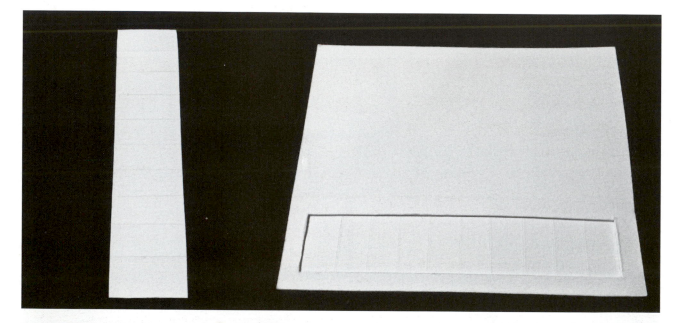

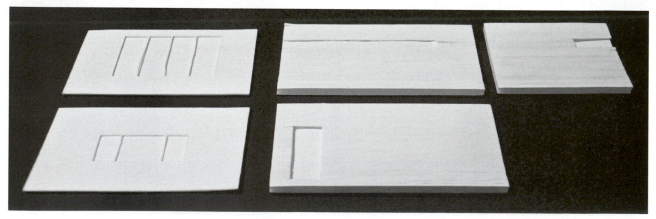

3. Use tacky glue to assemble the pieces of the model.
   - Set up a "dry run," making sure that you have all the pieces needed to create the final model before applying glue.

4. Repeat these steps to create the rest of the model.
   - Obviously, this can be a complex task to complete, but start at one corner and work your way out of the model.
   - Sections of the model may be removable in order to present options for portions of the design, such as different rooflines.

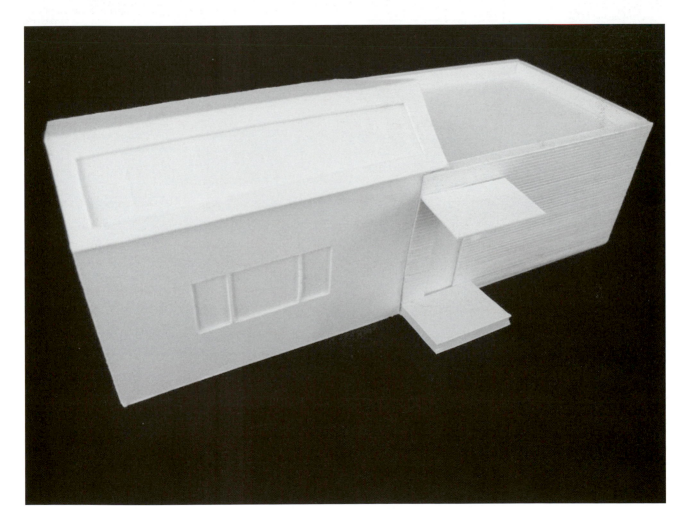

5. Finally, add a scaled figure, made out of foam-core board or a piece of wood, to represent a person in the space. The person should be about 5'-8" (at the scale in which the model was built) and placed next to, or within, the model.

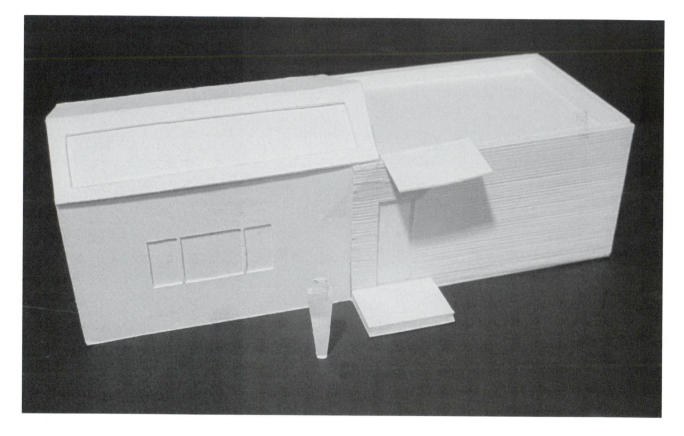

White models are a great tool to use to aid in understanding your design intent. They let everyone involved understand the design without any influence of material selection or color.

FINISH MODELS

Finish models are used to present a design to the client and potentially to be put on display. They are created to scale with products that represent the final material and finish selections. Every design detail may or may not be indicated, but the overall look and feel of the design will be communicated in a finish model.

Some companies have people in house who create these finish models, but a professional model builder can also be hired to produce them. In school, it is *your* job to create these models.

Finish models are typically constructed at the end of the design-development phase. In a freshman-level studio class, you may or may not create a finish model.

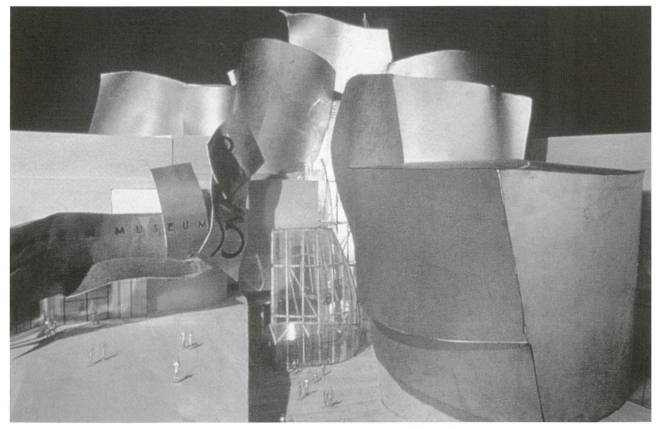

This model indicates the metal and glass used on the exterior of the museum and includes many scaled figures and signage.

A finish model indicates:

- The overall size and shape, or mass, of a building or object.

- The selected materials and finishes.

- An understanding of human scale. Multiple scaled figures (people) and items (cars, trees, furniture, etc.) should be placed in or around the model to demonstrate the relationship of the project to a person.

- Graphics and signage, if deemed necessary.

CREATING A FINISH MODEL

To create a finish model, you will follow the same steps as for a white model, but with a few differences:

1. You will use products that represent the materials and finishes selected for the project. This could include specialty papers, plastic, metal, or wood, any of which may need to be treated to achieve the desired effect.

2. Windows made from clear acetate or acrylic can be added. These materials are used to ensure that viewers understand that these sections of the model are glass, not just recesses or indentions in the surface. There are several ways to do this, and two are shown here.

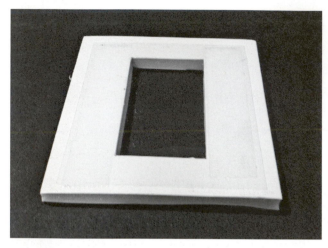

Acetate is cut to the same size as the entire wall and adhered with double-sided tape.

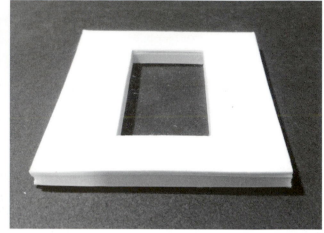

Acetate is sandwiched between foam-core board and museum board.

- Sandpaper is used on acetate to scuff up the surface, resulting in a piece that can be used to represent sandblasted or frosted glass in a model.

3. Finish models may include the addition of interior walls, doors, windows and openings, or other built-in components. This may also include plumbing fixtures, cabinetry, and, as in our one-bedroom cabin, fireplaces and shelving.

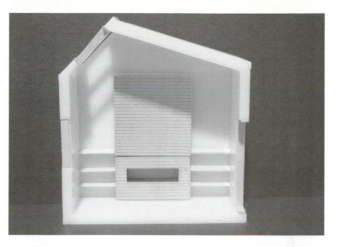

- Models can be built to separate, thereby showing different portions of the model.

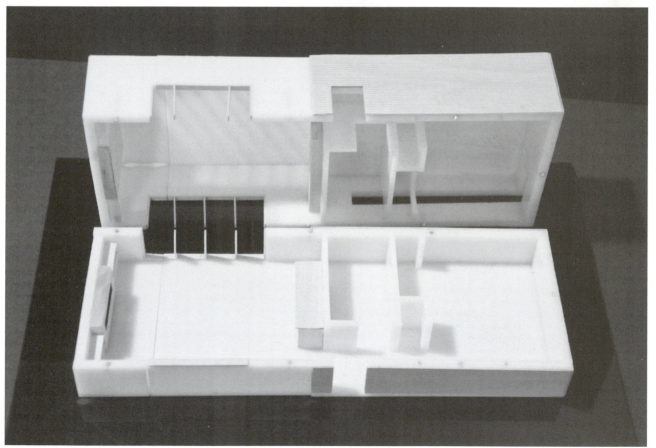

4. The addition of multiple scaled figures and items, such as trees, lamp posts, and furniture, makes the model more easily understood to the viewer. These objects can be made by hand or purchased from several websites or hobby stores. Here is an example showing the type of scaled trees and people that could be added to a finish model. Remember to always note the scale of the model when purchasing these items.
5. The physical site of the model is typically indicated as well to show the building or space in the context of its surroundings.

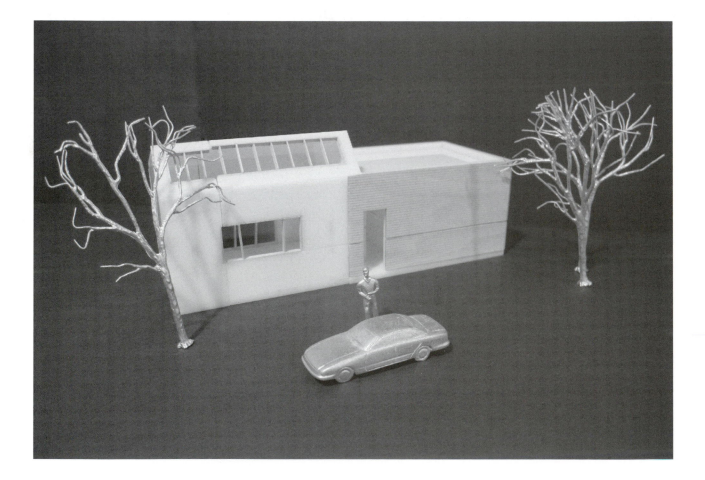

EXERCISE

IIIIIIIIIIIIIIIIIIIIIIIIIIIIIIIIIIIIIIIIIIIIIIIIIIIIIIIIIIIIIIIIIIIIIIIIIIIIIIIIIIIIIIIIIIIIIIIIIIIIIIIIIIIIIII

TOOLS NEEDED

Bone folder

Cork-backed ruler

Drafting dots

Foam-core board

Museum board

Pencil

Permanent marker

Self-healing mat

Tacky glue

X-acto knife

Set up your area and prepare to create four small 4" × 4" boxes using different assembling strategies. Place your self-healing mat on one side of your table for the cutting portion of the model-building exercise.

FOLDING STRATEGY

1. Cut three pieces of museum board: one at 3⅞" × 16¼" (the sides of the cube) and two at 4" × 4" (the top and bottom of the cube).

   - The narrower width of the side piece accommodates the thickness of the material of the top and bottom pieces in the dimensions of the cube. Think of the two 4"-square pieces as the floor and ceiling of the cube. The longer piece will become the walls.

   - Label each piece of board with a drafting dot and permanent marker, noting the name of the piece and/or the longest dimension, so that you can remember which piece is which when it comes time to assemble them. (This may seem elementary for this simple cube, but it will become a habit you appreciate when you build more complex models in the future.)

- Make sure that you measure twice and cut once. Use your scale to measure the board, and your cork-backed ruler and x-acto knife to cut the pieces. Keep the blade perpendicular to the piece of board you are cutting and snug against the cork-backed ruler.

2. Starting at one end of the $3\frac{7}{8}$" × $16\frac{1}{4}$" piece, make a mark at 4", 8", and 12" on the top and bottom edges of the strip. Create another mark $3\frac{15}{16}$" to the right of the 12" mark, producing a small strip at the end of the piece. This will become the glue tab once you have folded the board.

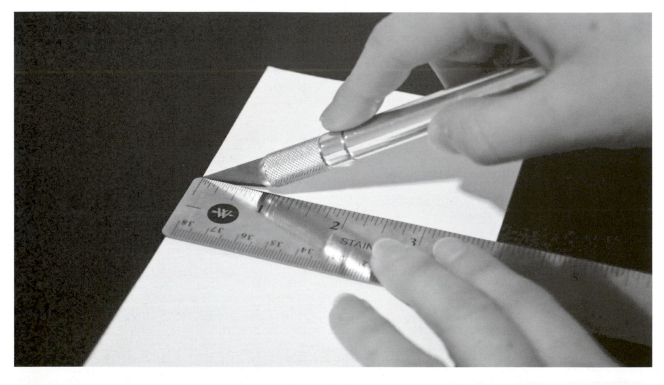

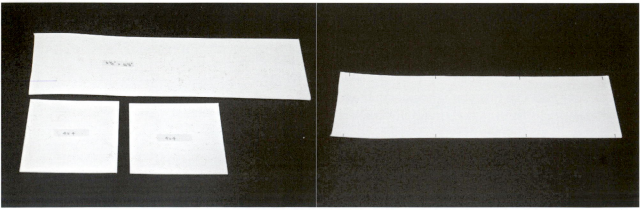

3. Create a score using the point of the bone folder at each set of marks, then use the side of the bone folder to form creases at the scores, creating the folds.

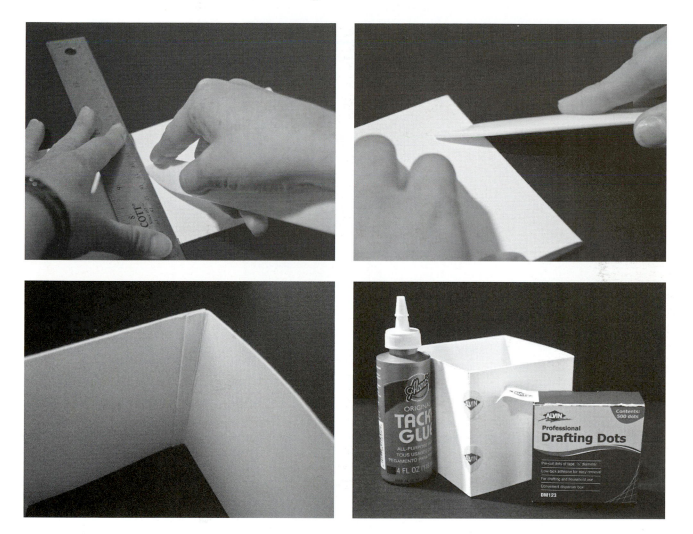

4. Stand the piece up, exposing the glue tab, and make sure that the corners are straight and true by holding each side. If one corner is not staying in place, you might have to crease it again. Then, glue the tab to the opposite end of the piece.

   - It is important to hold the piece together until the glue is thoroughly dry to ensure that it remains square. You can do this by using drafting dots at the joint and "propping up" each side with objects on hand.

5. Add the top and bottom pieces.

TIP: It is easier to add glue to the edges of the sides of the cube than to the surface of the top and bottom pieces.

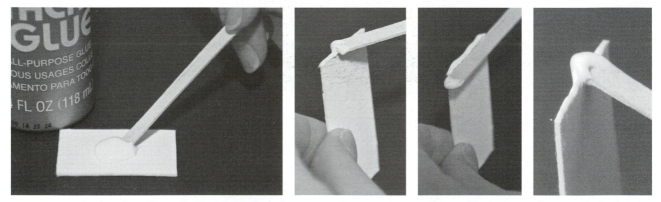

Do not apply the glue directly from the bottle. Instead, use a scrap piece of balsa wood to apply it. Dot the glue along the edge of the board, and then clean up the bead of glue by tapering it with an index card, an old business card, or a different piece of balsa wood.

CUT-PIECE STRATEGY

1. Cut four pieces of museum board at $3\frac{15}{16}$" × $3\frac{7}{8}$" and two pieces at 4" × 4".

    - Like the folding strategy, the different widths accommodate the thickness of the board in the dimensions of the cube.

    - Label each piece. In this case, label both 4" × 4" squares "A" and the four $3\frac{15}{16}$" × $3\frac{7}{8}$" pieces "B," with an arrow pointing in the lengthwise direction.

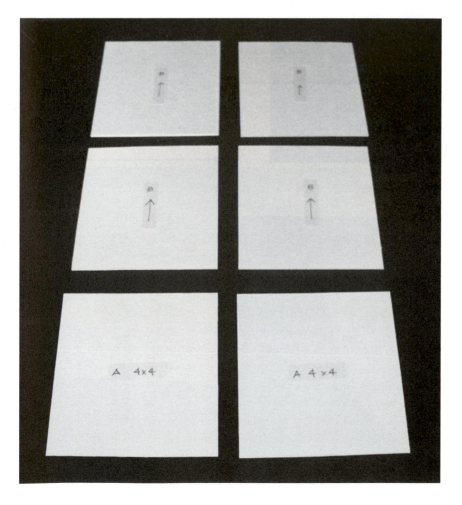

TIPS

- Make sure your cutting tool blade runs against the cork-backed ruler at a 90-degree angle to the material you are cutting. (This rule applies to every tool but the bevel tool.)
- Change a blade if it is producing rough edges when it cuts, and dispose of it properly.
- Adjust the marks and location of the cork-backed ruler to accommodate different tools.
- Always check the glue and the edges and corners of your board.
- Keep your work area clean.

EVALUATION

- Are all of your cubes square?
- Can you tell just by looking at your cuts when you did or did not change your blade?
- Did you use too much glue, or not enough?
- How is the overall craftsmanship? Are your pieces and final cubes clean and crisp?
- Did your skills improve with each cube you created?

SUMMARY

The ability to create a variety of three-dimensional models will make you a stronger designer. It is a skill that will serve you at every level in the design process, both in your studies and in your career.

APPENDIX

ORTHOGRAPHIC DRAWINGS

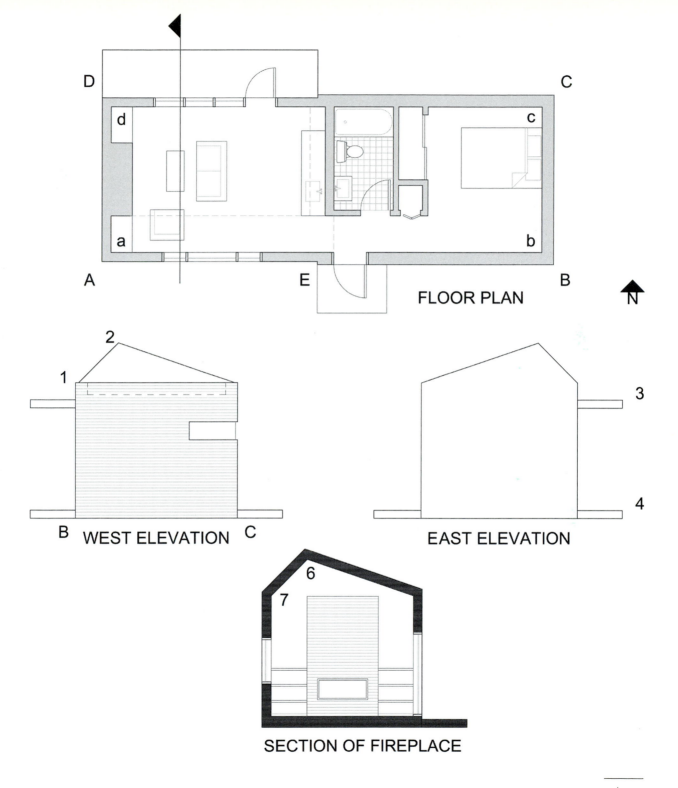

D

d

c

C

a

b

A

E

FLOOR PLAN

N

2

1

B   WEST ELEVATION   C

3

4

EAST ELEVATION

6

7

SECTION OF FIREPLACE

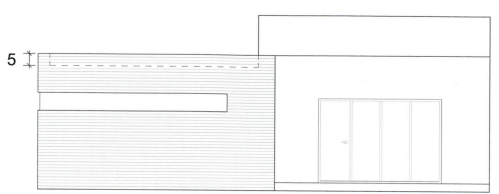

SOUTH ELEVATION

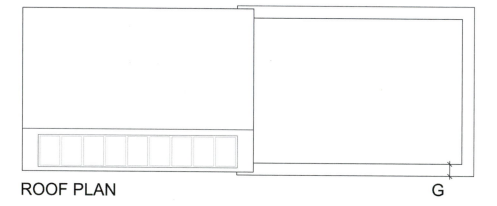

ROOF PLAN   G

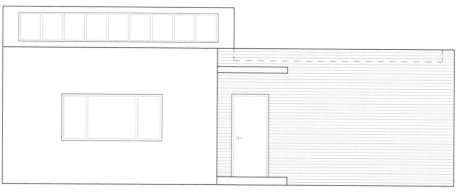

NORTH ELEVATION

BASIC METRIC CONVERSION TABLE

|||||||||||||||||||||||||||||||||||||||||||||||||||||||||||||||||||||||||||||||||||

DISTANCES

ENGLISH	METRIC
1 inch	2.54 centimeters
1 foot	0.3048 meter / 30.48 centimeters
1 yard	0.9144 meter

METRIC	ENGLISH
1 centimeter	0.3937 inch
1 meter	3.280 feet

WEIGHTS

ENGLISH	METRIC
1 ounce	28.35 grams
1 pound	0.45 kilogram

METRIC	ENGLISH
1 gram	0.035 ounce
1 kilogram	2.2 pounds

GENERAL FORMULA FOR CONVERTING:

Number of Units × Conversion Number = New Number of Units

TO CONVERT INCHES TO CENTIMETERS:

[number of inches] × 2.54 = [number of centimeters]

TO CONVERT CENTIMETERS TO INCHES:

[number of centimeters] × 0.3937 = [number of inches]

TO CONVERT FEET TO METERS:

[number of feet] × 0.3048 = [number of meters]

TO CONVERT METERS TO FEET:

[number of meters] × 3.280 = [number of feet]

TO CONVERT YARDS TO METERS:

[number of yards] × 0.9144 = [number of meters]

TO CONVERT OUNCES TO GRAMS:

[number of ounces] × 28.35 = [number of grams]

TO CONVERT GRAMS TO OUNCES:

[number of grams] × 0.035 = [number of ounces]

TO CONVERT POUNDS TO KILOGRAMS:

[number of pounds] × 0.45 = [number of kilograms]

TO CONVERT KILOGRAMS TO POUNDS:

[number of kilograms] × 2.2 = [number of pounds]

INDEX

||||||||||||||||||||||||||||||||||||||||||||||||||||||||||||||||||||||||||||||||||||||||||||||||||||||||||||||||||||||||||||||||

Acetate, 160, 184

Adhesive runners, 162

Architectural elements

    built-in shelving, 21, 124–26

    in isometric drawing, 11, 16

    in one-point perspective, 53, 63–65

    in two-point perspective, 113–25

Axonometric drawings, 6–24

    diametric, 6

    isometric, 6, 7–24

    trimetric, 6

Balsa wood, 159

Basswood, 159

Bevel (45-degree) cutter, 148, 150

Boards, 157–58

    See also Foam-core board

Bone folder, 163, 189

Building materials, 156–60

    metal, 160

    plastic, 160

    wood, 159

Cardboard, 157

Central axis of vision (CAV), 95, 97, 98

Chipboard, 158

The Chopper (cutting tool), 152

Circle cutters, 147, 150

Compass cutter, 147

Cone of vision (COV)

    in one-point perspective, 47

    in two-point perspective, 94

Craft knives, 143–44

Cut-piece strategy, 191–94

Cutting tools, 142–53

    The Chopper, 152

    circle cutters, 147

    craft knives, 143–44

    for foam-core board, 148–51

    mighty cutter, 152

    razor saw and miter box, 153

    rotary cutters, 147

    self-healing mats and, 154

    swivel knife, 146

    utility knives, 145

    wood-carving knife, 146

    x-acto knives, 143–44, 160, 188

Design development phase, 171

    white models in, 175

Diagonal point (DP), one-point

    perspective, 50

Diametric drawing, 6

Double-sided tape, 162

Drafting dots and tape, 54, 162

Dura-Lar, 160

Elevation oblique, 26
  steps in drafting, 34–36
Entourage, 75, 87
  in two-point perspective, 131–32
  See also Furniture; Human scale
Exterior isometric drawings, 9–15

Finish models, 181–86
  steps in creating, 183–85
Floor plan
  isometric drawing and, 10, 16
  plan oblique and, 28, 29
  in two-point perspective, 90, 92,
    98
Foam-core board, 157
  cutting tools for, 147, 148–51
FoamWerks cutting tools, 149–51
45-degree (bevel) cutter, 148
Folding strategy, 187–90
  bone folder and, 163, 189
Freestyle cutter, 151
Furniture
  in one-point perspective, 53, 75–76
  in plan oblique, 32
  round objects, 79–80
  in two-point perspective, 131–33

Gehry, Frank, 169, 172
  See also Guggenheim Museum
Glue, for model building, 148, 161–62,
    179
  in folding strategy, 189, 190
  hot-glue guns, 162
  Tacky glue, 161, 179
Ground line (GL)
  in one-point perspective, 48
  in two-point perspective, 98, 112,
    113, 121

Guggenheim Museum (Bilbao, Spain),
    169, 172
  finish model of, 181
  rip-and-tear models of, 172
Hole drill, 151
Horizon line (HL)
  one-point perspective, 49
  in two-point perspective, 98–99, 112
Hot-glue guns, 162
Human scale
  in finish model, 182
  in one-point perspective, 44, 77
  in two-point perspective, 89
  white model building and, 176, 180

Interior isometric drawing, 17–24
Isometric drawing, 6, 7–24
  exterior, 9–15
  features of, 7
  interior, 17–24
  perspective drawing compared, 44
  steps in creating, 8

Knives. *See* Cutting tools

Left measuring point (LMP), 96, 97, 112,
    114
Left vanishing point (LVP), 95, 97, 112,
    114, 116
Line weights, 24, 33
  in one-point perspective, 78
  in two-point perspective, 134
Logan Graphic Products. *See*
    FoamWerks cutting tools

Massing models, 171
  See also Rip-and-tear models
Matboard, 157

Measurement document, 98

Measuring line. *See* Vertical measuring line

Measuring points (MP), 95, 96, 97, 112, 114
  intersection with vanishing points, 102

Metal, for model building, 160

Metric conversion table, 205–6

Mighty cutter, 152

Miter box, 153

Miter-joint corners, 148

Model-building strategies, 166–95
  cut-piece strategy, 191–94
  finish models, 181–86
  folding strategy, 187–90
  rip-and-tear models, 171–74
  technologies and, 170
  tips and evaluation, 194
  white models, 175–80

Model-building tools, 140–65
  building materials, 156–60
  cutting tools, 142–53
  paper for, 156
  self-healing mats, 154
  supplies and, 161–63
  tool storage, 164
  triangles and rulers, 155
  See also Cutting tools

Museum board, 158
  white models and, 175

Oblique drawings, 25–36
  elevation oblique, 26, 34–36
  plan oblique, 25, 27–33

One-point perspective, 40–85
  adding architectural elements, 63–70
  adding built-in elements, 59–62
  adding depth and detail in, 71–74

adding furniture and people, 75–78
  adding round objects in, 79–81
  creating, 45
  drawing in, 54–78
  evaluation, 84
  features of, 44
  steps in drafting, 46–52
  tips for, 83

Orthographic drawings, 4, 196–203
  isometric drawing and, 8, 10
  one-point perspective and, 46
  paraline drawings and, 3, 5
  plan oblique and, 28
  two-point perspective and, 113, 121

Paper, for model building, 156

Paraline drawings, 2–39
  axonometric drawings, 6–24
  components of, 5
  definition of, 3
  oblique drawings, 25–36
  tips and evaluation, 38

Perspective.
    See One-point perspective;
    Two-point perspective

Picture plane (PP)
  in one-point perspective, 46
  in two-point perspective, 93

Plan oblique, 25, 27–33
  creating, 28
  features of, 27
  steps in drafting, 29–33

Plastic, for model building, 160

PP. *See* Picture plane

Rabbet cutter, 148, 150, 193

Razor saw and miter box, 153

Right measuring point (RMP), 96, 97, 112

Right vanishing point (RVP), 95, 97, 112, 127

Rip-and-tear models, 171–74
    steps in creating, 173–74
    white models compared to, 176

Roof elements, in isometric drawing, 12

Rotary cutters, 147

Round objects, adding, 79–81

Ruler, cork-backed, 155

Scale, 48

Schematic design phase, 171

Section line, 17

Self-healing mats, 154

Station point (SP)
    one-point perspective, 46, 47
    in two-point perspective, 94

Straight cutter, 150

Study models, 171
    See also Rip-and-tear models

Swivel knife, 146

Tacky glue, 161, 179

Tape, for model building, 162

Three-dimensional models.
    See Model-building strategies

Tools. *See* Cutting tools; Model-building tools

Tool storage, 164

Triangle, 13, 30, 35, 51, 155

Trimetric drawing, 6

Two-point perspective, 86–139
    adding depth and detail to, 129–30
    adding entourage to, 131–32
    additional vanishing point in, 88
    architectural elements in, 113–25
    built-in shelving in, 124–25
    creating, 90–91
    drawing in, 112–34
    evaluation, 138
    exercise, 135–36
    features of, 89
    floor plane in, 101–3
    front corner in, 100
    steps in drafting, 92–111
    tips for, 137

Utility knives, 145

Vanishing point, 41
    left vanishing point, 95, 97, 112, 114, 116
    in one-point perspective, 43, 50
    right vanishing point, 95, 97, 112, 127

Vertical measuring line (VML), 98, 105, 112, 116, 122

V-groove cutter, 150

White models, 175–80
    steps in creating, 177–80

Wood, in model building
    balsa wood and basswood, 159

Wood-carving knife, 146

X-acto knives, 143–44, 160, 188
    utility knives compared, 145